£3.49
WK 10

D1576752

THE
OPTIMIST'S
HANDBOOK

Facts, figures and arguments to silence cynics,
doom-mongers and defeatists

BY

NICK INMAN

Harriman House Ltd
3A Penns Road
Petersfield
Hampshire
GU32 2EW

Tel. +44 (0)1730 233870
Fax +44 (0)1730 233880
Email: enquiries@harriman-house.com
Website: www.harriman-house.com

First published in Great Britain in 2007 by Harriman House Ltd.
Copyright © Harriman House Ltd

The right of Nicholas Inman to be identified as the author has
been asserted in accordance with the Copyright, Design and
Patents Act 1988.

ISBN 1-905-64129-X
ISBN13 978-1-905641-29-1

British Library Cataloguing in Publication Data
A CIP catalogue record for this book can be obtained from the
British Library.

Printed and bound by Biddles Ltd, Kings Lynn, Norfolk.

Non si male nunc et olim sic erit

(If things are bad now
they won't always be)

Horace, Odes II

About the author

Nick Inman was born in Yorkshire in 1956 and studied politics at the University of Bristol in the 1970s before becoming a travel writer specialising in Spain. He is married with two children and lives in southwest France.

Acknowledgements

Many people contributed ideas or information that helped shape this book and to all of them I am grateful. In particular, I would like to thank Steve Eckett for leads that took me into interesting areas that I might not otherwise have thought about; Josefina Fernandez; Philip Jenks, who challenged me to explain myself while editing the book; Richard Kelly; Ben Soffa, Press Officer for the Campaign for Nuclear Disarmament (CND); Clara Villanueva; and Stewart Wild for his serendipitous supplies of cuttings.

Another person I would have liked to have thanked for general inspiration and for reminding me never to be complacent is Charles Clasen, who died while this book was being written.

For my mother

Contents

Introduction

Miserable world, wouldn't you say? Switch on the news and it's all war, crime, starvation and economic crisis. And now we have climate change to really throw us into panic: there are too many people on earth and we are polluting ourselves to death.

Miserable life, if it comes to that. We put a brave face on it and pretend we're having fun but we spend most of our time doing things we don't want to do. And for what? However you look at it, your life is a short, speeded-up, pointless film which can only have one unhappy ending.

Perhaps I shouldn't have been surprised, then, at people's reactions when I told them I was writing a book about optimism. Often they'd step back – and look concerned, as if I had taken on the impossible. How could anybody be an optimist in a world full of so much suffering? What would I find to say? Presumably I'd have to lie, exaggerate or at the very least keep my comments vague?

Let's straighten a few things out right away. Bad things happen all the time. Life is, as one of Jung's patients put it, a terminal illness with no prospect of remission; and it is unfair. The longest-term prognostic for humanity, the planet and the universe is prima facie not good. Scientists foresee only increasing entropy (as featured in the Second Law of Thermodynamics): the dispersal or loss of energy of the system causing an increase in disorder and disintegration until the Whole Thing goes "phutt". You can see it for yourself: when did rust, dust, rot and decay ever take a holiday? Or ask any gardener, who will tell you bluntly that you can spend 24 hours a day outdoors with hoes, forks, shears, secateurs, blow torches and noxious chemical agents but the ivy and the bindweed will still eventually win.

And, looking around, it is not hard to argue that the world is going to hell whether we like it or not. This may not be an entirely accurate verdict. Nothing in this book is meant to deny that tragedies, minor and major, happen every day to individuals, communities, countries and civilisations. Before we draw damning conclusions, however, we must be sure that we are seeing reality straight and there are several reasons why we can easily fool ourselves that things are worse than they are:

1. We only see a small part of the world with our own eyes but we form judgements about life, the universe and everything based on what we see on television or the internet, read in the papers, hear on the radio or are told by other people. Second-hand, in other words.

2. We enjoy hearing and telling horror stories more than feel-good ones. We're suckers for *schadenfreude* but have little time for tales of ordinary success and achievement. We therefore get the impression that there is far more bad than good at large in the world.

3. There are powerful groups which have an interest in telling us that we are in an anxious, nervous or depressed rather than a satisfied state. Politicians know that a scared electorate is a supine electorate. For newspaper editors, bad news is good news – for sales. Multinational companies know that the best

way to stimulate demand for their products is to play on our inadequacies. None of these entities benefit from our contentment.

4. We are victims of our own ideologies, adapting facts (or ignoring them) to suit our prejudices. If we don't like the colour of the government, we see everything it does as wrong, whatever the truth.

5. We are superstitious. We secretly fear that building up our hopes will invite the gods to bring them crashing down. If we expect the worst, we will never be disappointed.

6. We like fixed prescriptions. We don't like to be reminded that things are in constant flux, that trends can be reversed, and that we may need to revise the judgement we arrived at yesterday.

7. We are loathe to admit that nothing is as simple as it seems. We don't like having to add nuances to our black and white preconceptions.

8. We have a pathological tendency to shift responsibility and shirk blame. There is nothing we can do personally about the events that shape the world; everything is the fault of 'them'; and 'they' are everything that we are not: corrupt, selfish, greedy, deceitful and untrustworthy.

As the director and producer Alejandro Jodorowsky put it: "reality is a huge plate of food. And depending on the kind of mouth you have, you'll feed yourself accordingly. In other words, you give the food its taste. The food itself has no taste. If your mouth tastes chicken, reality is a chicken."

But if we are to make any sense of the world we need to recognise these distorting filters for what they are and make an effort to see a balanced picture of reality. We must confront the negative but also allow ourselves also to see the positive. "If way to the better there be," said Thomas Hardy, "it exacts a full look at the worst".

Optimism is a tool for rebalancing the picture of reality we make in our heads. Its objective is not to arrive at the artificially buoyant, lighter-than-air, rose-spectacled, chin-upping conclusion of the Victorian governess who "when the weather was bad, was still thankful because it was better than none at all", but to enable us to stop complaining and take action.

Optimism is an attitude. It is not a prediction or a mathematical formula. It speaks in the language of probability rather than certainty; it is a disposition to assess a situation and keep walking with hope – because hope there always is – rather than to sit down and cry.

When Robinson Crusoe is coming to terms with being shipwrecked, and he finds himself wavering between the urge to survive and the temptation to crumple in despair, he decides to let reason be the judge. He makes two lists of the encouraging/discouraging aspects of his situation – just the facts as he sees them, without emotion – and comes to the logical conclusion that, on balance, he should be grateful he is still alive, not in immediate danger and well supplied with the provisions he needs to sustain him until he is rescued. That is optimism.

The editor-at-large of *Wired* magazine, Kevin Kelly, summed this approach up for a survey of scientific thinkers carried out by *The Edge* website in January 2007:

"…on average and over time, the new solutions slightly outweigh the new problems. As Rabbi Zalman Schacter-Shalomi once said, 'There is more good than evil in the world—but not by much.' Unexpectedly 'not much' is all that is needed when you have the power of compound interest at work – which is what culture is. The world needs to be only 1% (or even one-tenth of 1%) better day in and day out to accumulate civilization. As long as we create 1% more than we destroy each year, we have progress. This delta is so small that it is almost imperceptible, particularly in the face of the 49% of death and destruction that is in our face. Yet this tiny, slim, and shy differential generates progress."

We have a choice between writing humanity off as a basket case or investing in this 'positive margin' and earning a modest rate of compound interest as hope wins over cynicism; intelligence over stupidity; empathy over selfishness; and courage over denial. Progress is often slow and unspectacular, but any rate of forward motion is enough.

If we face the most intractable problems of the world – terrorism, war, poverty – with the expectation that solutions can be found, life becomes a 'positive sum game', with everyone winning. Paraphrasing a famous speech given by John F. Kennedy in 1963, the economist Jeffrey Sachs appealed to a radio audience in 2007: "if we believe that war is inevitable we will end up at war. If we believe that extreme poverty can't be solved we will end up letting millions and millions of people die."

Optimism is thus the quality of the activist, the campaigner, the world-changer. As a disposition towards co-operation, compromise, construction, changing an enemy through force of argument rather than force of arms, it offers an alternative to the politics of division, confrontation, complacency, exploitation and short-termism.

If that is not enough to convince you to convert to optimism, let me appeal to your self-interest. Studies have shown that optimists are better equipped than pessimists to recognise and adapt to 'negative' information and to take action to avoid risk or danger. They also tend to rebound faster from bad luck and setbacks which they are likely to reclassify as challenges. Again, these studies suggest that optimism is good for your health. If we accept that there is a link between mind and body (even if we can't define it), would it be so surprising to be told that optimism has a physical effect on your cells and boosts your immune system? Optimists cope better with suffering and know that despair serves no useful purpose. If you have to live with pain or struggle, with depression, or to overcome enormous difficulty, optimism is really your only option. One of the most eloquent essays on optimism ever written is by Helen Keller who was born deaf and blind but who went on to contribute more to the world than many people born with all their senses intact.

Pessimists, on the other hand, are more likely to underachieve because they have less motivation; they are likely to take less care of themselves; and more prone to accidents – they almost literally walk into them.

Pessimistic children are less likely to grow into healthy adults and live fulfilled lives. If our social and education policies should have one aim only it must be to give young people a sense that there are values and goals worth striving for; nihilism is the easy but senseless road to nowhere.

Subjects and themes

The book consists of a series of topics arranged alphabetically (although they can be read in any order) about which there is something positive to say. Most of these topics are intended to convey serious information but a few have been included for light relief from what might otherwise be a relentless catalogue of worthy thinking. Some tackle more ethereal themes which, it seems to me, an optimist has an obligation to address: whether we can trust human nature; whether we can predict the future with any accuracy; the difference between optimism and hope; the nature of happiness; and – how can we ignore it? – the meaning of life.

The choice of what is and is not included is necessarily subjective but the reasons for optimism in each case are based on fact and argument. Without specifically intending it, I am aware that I have cast two major protagonists in the book – humanity and the earth – and two minor ones: you and me. All four are connected and part of a seamless whole, the universe, which gets its own mention at the very end.

Inevitably, those of us who live in the rich countries of the west have more reasons to feel optimistic than those who live in what are called developing countries; but I don't think the situation is quite so clear cut as this statement suggests. It is a mistake to think too much in terms of 'us' and 'them', of one world separated into distinct economic blocs. Every country is unique and, within it, every individual is different from all the rest. Even though it is obvious that a large proportion of humanity doesn't share your or my good fortune, much of what I have to say is of universal relevance.

I have not set out to deliver any particular message other than that optimism offers a more accurate and useful view of reality than pessimism, but certain themes seem to recur in the material and these are worth summarising:

- **We need to see the big and small picture at the same time.** We may be impressed by the grand sweeps of history, and it may be easier to think about humanity in generalisations, but we mustn't forget that the whole is made up of parts. If we limit ourselves to a galactic overview of life on earth, we miss the billions of individual stories that are just as worthy of our attention. We must, of course, take an interest in what governments, multinational companies and international organisations get up to but we should not forget the role played by ordinary people at ground level. People without power or affiliation do change the world sometimes; a lone campaigner can articulate the mood of millions; and social, technological and economic movements often rise from small-scale endeavours that are dismissed in their infancy as one-off, localised experiments of no universal importance. It's easy to belittle any success story as being of relevance to only one family, one village, one moment in time. But a lesson learnt in one part of the globe can spread everywhere else with telepathic velocity.

- **We shouldn't swallow everything that the mass media wants to feed us.** What we see on television is a representation of reality, not reality itself. We must always look behind and beyond what we are told by busy journalists whose interests may not coincide with our own.

- **We shouldn't be over-demanding.** We may sneer at a one percent cut in poverty as being too little too late but it is a movement in the right direction which records a significant improvement in the lives of almost 10 million individual men, women, boys, girls and babies.

- **We must learn to think in the long term.** Consumerism encourages us to think of ourselves and our own short-term needs but the future extends beyond tomorrow and next week. We can live well in the present and plan for the wellbeing of future generations simultaneously.

- **Everything is connected.** Problems seldom exist in isolation and it pays to observe how one thing relates to another before we prescribe solutions. The upside of this is that a solution to one problem can set off a virtuous chain-reaction which clears up several other problems as well.

- **Diversity is desirable.** After a 20th century rife with dogmatic political and economic one-size-fits-all 'unified field theories', we should be wary of all ideology, centralised planning and blanket solutions. There may be many different ways to address what seems like a common problem and each individual, each community must be allowed to take his/its own approach. As a corollary we should be wary of thinking that we see the problem better from outside than do those at the sharp end.

- **We must be alive to potential as much as to actuality;** the latent can become a potent force if it is given the chance to manifest itself. We need to spread opportunity through the world and give it time to flourish.

- **We should respect but not revere science**, or, more exactly, the conviction that rationality and empiricism are the only sources of knowledge. This is not an argument in favour of superstition. Our current intellectual challenge is to accept evidence as the basis of knowledge and the precursor of decision and action, but to find a place for 'inner evidence' such as that provided by our emotions, ethics and intuition. The two can co-exist.

If "history is a race between education and catastrophe", as H.G. Wells saw it, we could say the same of the future. We've got much to learn, as individuals and as a species, but essentially we're keeping pace with the curriculum. If we keep turning up to class with an optimistic outlook, who knows what problems we may overcome and what we may achieve.

Altruism

The Nobel Laureate economist Gary Becker argues that people always act in their own economic self-interest and that the only surprising thing is that some romanticists don't accept selfishness as the root or sole motivator of human society. But there is at least one other stimulus to action which is hard to fit into conventional economic or scientific theory: altruism, behaving in the best interests of others at the expense of one's own. The question is – does anyone really act altruistically?

According to Darwinian theory the only exceptions to outright competition for survival and the pick of the best mating partners are 'kinship' or 'reciprocal' altruism – calculated generosity towards anyone who, respectively, shares your genes or is likely to scratch your back in return. To this extent only, our brains are 'wired for empathy'.

But there are instances of selfless behaviour which are hard to explain. In the Second World War, many gentiles in Nazi occupied countries harboured Jews because they felt it was the right thing to do even if their own lives were endangered. The most famous example is that of Oskar Schindler who saved over 1,000 Jewish workers from the extermination camps: "I knew the people who worked for me," he later explained. "When you know people, you have to behave toward them like human beings."

Another example was given by Ian Linden, director of the Catholic Institute for International Relations, who had this to say in a BBC radio programme:

"I've worked, in the past, with missionaries in Zimbabwe during the war years when the Zandler forces were coming to power and I remember very clearly a mission priest saying, 'oh you go in the second car, I'll go in the first car', and the first time I wondered what on earth is that all about? And it was of course that the first car hits the mine in the road and the second car didn't. And he did it as sort of simply as somebody might usher you through a door. It was absolutely unconscious, it wasn't a big deal. It was just that I was a visitor, he lived there all the time, he was a missionary and if anybody was going to go up in the air, you know with losing their legs and so on, it was going to be him and not me and anyway his interpretation of what his life should be was the sort of person that says you go in the second car…"

It's not hard to find many, less extreme examples of altruism in everyday life. Anyone who gives their time and energy to campaign for a cause – animal rights or poverty in the third world – could be said to be acting altruistically. All vocational jobs – teaching, nursing and the like – require at least a little altruism. And there are heroic individuals who stand up to bullies and thugs even if they risk getting beaten or stabbed themselves.

There are also altruists in politics – we think of them as statesmen rather than politicians – and in business when profits are amassed in order to be given away philanthropically (Schindler, of course, was a businessman who depleted his own fortune on behalf of 'his' Jews).

And you could say downsizing environmentalists – people who 'deny' themselves the luxury of filling their wheelie bins with waste packaging and who reduce their carbon footprint to the minimum – are the new altruists.

Many cases of supposed altruism can be explained away by other motives: service, duty, guilt, the need to be liked or even noticed, and a cynic might say that altruists are always in it for selfish gain, however abstruse: they are 'buying pleasure' or 'winning' a do-good feeling or even, if they are religiously motivated, saving their own souls in the hereafter.

Kristen Renwick Monroe, author of *The Heart of Altruism*, is dismissive of the hidden motive theories. Individuals who act altruistically, she says, seldom reflect on what they are doing before and during the act: they merely see their range of options and do what they think needs to be done.

No one is suggesting that we should all behave selflessly all the time – although, according to Confucius, that is the only way to make civilisation work properly – but perhaps we should give altruists more credit and recognition, and try to be a little more generous and empathetic ourselves. We could also teach altruism as a social good, although this would undoubtedly distort the working of the free market. But for now and tomorrow, let's just be glad that some people don't just think about themselves.

Sources

The Heart of Altruism: Perceptions of a Common Humanity, by Kristen Renwick Monroe (1998)

Anaesthetics

If you are one of life's habitual complainers, consider for a moment a world in which there are no drugs to provide relief from cuts, migraines, toothache, disease, viruses and other common ailments. Not to mention surgery. Anaesthetics haven't been around all that long but they have made an incalculable difference to our attitude to healthcare.

In the early 19th century, a surgeon amputating a limb had no choice but to do so with the patient conscious, drugged only with a little brandy or morphine. It wasn't unusual for a victim to die of the shock.

Anaesthetics only began to be used from around 1850 and it was not until the 1950s that patients could be put to sleep using drugs which were easy to control. Now, medicine can deploy a range of local and general anaesthetics for interventions major, minor and elective, even if what is being pumped into us are still essentially poisonous cocktails.

In the future there are likely to be further refinements to anaesthetics to speed up recovery times and manage pain better. Maybe, too, some new, non-chemical anaesthetic technique will be discovered, reducing risks and side-effects still further.

Appropriate technology

In 1991, Trevor Baylis, swimming pool installer, erstwhile escapologist and would-be inventor, was watching television when he found himself mesmerized by a documentary on the spread of Aids in Africa. A field-worker was explaining that the best way to stop the disease would be to broadcast information about it on the radio – but how could poor people in rural areas listen to the radio when a set of batteries cost more than a family's weekly food bill?

This programme impelled Baylis into his workshop where he designed a prototype clockwork powered radio which when cranked by hand for two minutes would provide 14 minutes of listening time. The idea was as simple as it was ingenious. The user wound a steel spring and this, as it uncoiled, drove a generator. Because the energy was saved in a physical form (the spring) the radio could be built to be robust and long lasting; to be transported to remote places over rough roads, stored for years if necessary and still work perfectly. After an appearance on the BBC's *Tomorrow's World*, Baylis found the backing he needed to go into production and the first commercial wind-up radio went on sale in 1996.

This is a perfect example of 'appropriate technology' in action: the application of the most cost-effective, least environmentally damaging level of technology to meet a particular purpose.

The term is almost always used in connection with developing countries, and particularly rural areas without electricity or other infrastructure. Appropriate technology is meant to enable poor countries to 'leapfrog' to a higher level of development with minimum investment, pollution and waste.

But we in the developed world could do with applying the concept to our own lifestyles. Imagine if cars, computers, fridges and the rest could be made only as complicated as they needed to be, without additional features; if their mechanics were transparent and fixable by anyone with a basic set of tools; if their running and maintenance costs were low; and if they were built to last rather than to be thrown away at the first malfunction.

Other items of appropriate technology in use in developing countries include:

- *The Universal Malian Nut Sheller,* invented by the American film technician and aid worker Jock Brandis after a visit to Mali. A woman there asked him to look for a cheap machine to shell peanuts when he got back to the USA but as he couldn't find an existing one, Brandis created a low-cost, hand-operated one to do the job.

- *The Jhai PC,* a solid-state, low energy consuming computer which is powered by a foot crank mounted on a bicycle frame: quite literally, you have to do some footwork to download your emails. It was originally created for poor villages in Laos by the Jhai Foundation but both the software and hardware are open source and that sums up the philosophy of most appropriate technology inventions.

- *The Loband website* which renders complicated pages as simple text for those with slow internet access (and, let's face it, much of the time the images and the graphics don't add anything to the contents).

- *The 'zeer' refrigerator,* a clay pot within a clay pot, invented by Mohammed Bah Abba in 1995.
- *'Fog collecting',* the delightfully named technique in which water is taken from the air by condensing it on a piece of canvas and letting it flow into a trough.
- *The Roundabout Playpump,* a water pump powered by children playing.
- *The Hippo Water Roller,* a way of rolling water along the ground instead of lugging it on shoulders or head.
- *The Lifestraw.* Not dissimilar to the sort of drinking straw that western children clamour for but functionally about as far from it as you can get. This is a mini-water purification plant which allows the user to drink unclean water. It is powered by sucking.
- *Reedbed sewage systems,* a natural way of cleaning up waste water
- *The Whirlwind Wheelchair,* an inexpensive open-source convenience for disabled people without money.

Not all these items are low-cost or applicable to all developing countries but they show how ingenuity can lead to simple solutions for common problems. In some cases, the spur to invention and manufacture has been profit, in others the challenge of solving a social ill.

Sources

Practical Action: www.practicalaction.org

Architecture, *ecological*

The kind of architecture we always hear about, the kind that makes the headlines and that endures for centuries, is the grand, civic, religious, corporate, aristo-royal stuff; but the kind that really matters is the stuff we live in. We're likely to see two important trends in vernacular architecture continuing into the near future, one a step forward and one a step back.

The step back is to realize that our ancestors knew what they were doing. Before the mass production of identical little boxes made of ticky-tack, people learned how to build houses the hard way, by living in them for a few centuries. They paid more attention to tempering the effects of prevailing winds when choosing a site than getting a good view and they used locally-available materials to their best advantage. There is now a movement 'back' to natural building in which pre-formed blocks, cement, PVC, fibre-glass and other similar materials are eschewed in favour of stone, timber, lime mortar and natural insulating materials. Houses built with natural materials are said to be healthier to live in; they are certainly more pleasing to look at, inside and out.

The step forward is to incorporate modern techniques of energy efficiency into houses, thereby making them more comfortable to live in while reducing utility bills and easing the strain on the environment.

A good, or at least, well-intentioned example of commercial eco-building is BedZED, the Beddington Zero Energy Development, a carbon-neutral eco-housing community built in Surrey in 2002 by the Peabody Trust. Natural, reclaimed or recycled materials were used wherever possible and energy efficiency integrated into the plans – the houses face south for 'passive solar gain' and their walls store heat up when it's warm and release it when it's cold. Renewable energy is used to provide power; rainwater is collected and recycled.

As natural house building and renovation become more common, prices will fall and there's no reason why the principles shouldn't be used to build energy-frugal, sustainable ecocities or ecopolises in the future.

Sources

The Natural House Book, by David Pearson (1998)

"*An optimist is a person who sees a green light everywhere, while a pessimist sees only the red stoplight. . . The truly wise person is colorblind.*"

Albert Schweitzer

Awareness, *environmental*

The aim of Live Earth, a series of pan-continental rock concerts in July 2007, was to raise awareness of the world's environmental problems. While critics complained about the amount of energy expended to get already carbon-profligate performers on to the various stages, the organisers claimed that the extra pollution was justifiable if it made millions of people change their lifestyles. "More people feel that dog mess and litter are problems than the destruction of the habitability of the only planet human beings have," explained former US vice president Al Gore, one of the promoters of the project. "We treat the atmosphere of the earth as an open sewer. … CO_2 is odourless, invisible and tasteless, and has its pernicious effect only in the global dimension."

Environmental awareness is always a good thing – even if you dissent from the climate change consensus – but Live Earth might have achieved more had it been able to show rock stars living sustainable but still exciting lives. A concert set beside a compost heap (sponsored by some cool brand of biodegradable soft drink) would have set the right example, as would publicity pictures showing today's stars living in Bohemian profligacy but still taking out their recycling bins and cycling to their recording studios.

Still, eco-awareness is seeping into the human consciousness in the same way that rock stars have generally learned to adopt less self-destructive habits and the rest of us have come to see smoking and drink driving as anti-social, killer habits rather than the height of rebellious sophistication. It's good that we are beginning to take responsibility for our energy consumption and the pollution we directly and indirectly cause. We're starting to see that managing our lifestyles is not that difficult or time consuming.

Of course, we can always do more and maybe we will all gradually have to follow the example of those humble, pioneering individuals (not rock stars) who recycle their waste to the degree that they don't even own wheelie bins, and who catch trains to cross continents, not planes. It would take just one international celebrity to adopt these habits for carbon neutrality, green motoring and sustainable living to become the next 'must-have' fashions.

The best of all possible worlds

Gottfried Wilhelm Leibniz (1646-1716), a German polymath who wrote in Latin and French, was the original 'walking encyclopedia' and a superstar in the days when celebrities were expected to have beautiful minds rather than beautiful bodies. He is credited with the invention of optimism (which Voltaire satirises in his novel *Candide*).

According to Leibniz's 'Principle of Sufficient Reason', there has to be a logical reason why things are as they are, and Man can work this out for himself. If God is perfect, Leibniz argues in *Essais de Théodicée* (1710), He wouldn't be capable of creating a second-rate world. Or, to be more exact, if He had to decide which to create out of an infinite number of possible worlds (any of which would have to be imperfect, as it was separate from Himself) He would opt for the least imperfect – that is, the best of all possible worlds. In this world there would be the optimum ratio of good to evil. That, according to Leibniz, is the world we inhabit, and since it is the best possible world, we should feel confident in its essential goodness.

Of course, the best way to prove Leibniz wrong would be to point to a world which is better, or worse, than this one.

Body, *your*

There are 100 trillion cells in your body arranged in 12 principal interconnected systems of staggering complexity. The whole thing runs without the aid of batteries on a huge variety of different fuels and will continue to function well even when pushed to its limits or misused.

It is a miracle that any of your organs work at all. They keep going by themselves every day during your whole life, starting from the second you breathe the air outside your mother. Even more incredibly, they work all together at the same time, without getting in the way of each other, and they grow up with you.

During your life you will spend:

- ⧗ three and half years eating, putting your digestive track to intensive use;

- ⧗ eight years (only?) working, straining your brain or brawn or both;

- ⧗ six months clenching and unclenching your sphincter on the toilet;

- ⧗ twelve years ruining your posture in front of the television;

- ⧗ another twelve years talking your jaw off.

Your legs, meanwhile, will clock up 22,000 km before they are done.

And your body will go on working at some level at least right up until the second you die. A spent capsule, it then spontaneously disintegrates and recycles itself.

So what if you have got a few aches and pains, if you don't like your nose, and whine about having to wear glasses? We're all miracles of biological engineering, and we shouldn't forget it.

Book, *the survival of the*

Most of us use books and computers every day, and wouldn't want to have to do without either. The two serve different purposes and provide different pleasures; and whereas no library on earth could supply browsers (in the old sense) with half the contents of the internet, the internet can and probably one day will provide browsers (in the new sense) with the contents of every library on earth. There is a danger, therefore, that the book will gradually give up the struggle with digitalia and one day soon we'll be reading everything on screens.

A love of books may betray a sentimental, antiquated, generational attachment – until a decade ago there was no other in-depth source of information about history and far away places – but it may also be an indication that the medium works. Some technologies meet a need and serve a purpose without fuss, and that's why they are popular and enduring.

Techophiles seem to see the book as a challenge. Surely it can be bettered by an electronic gadget, they insist. But sometimes we look for the new to prove what we can do, not because of what it can do for us. Once we dreamed of a paperless office and anyone who predicts the death of the book should ask themselves why it hasn't happened yet.

'E-paper' will undoubtebly improve and you will one day be able to carry the entire opus of English, French and Spanish literature to the beach on a device hanging from your keychain. But the book is not a competitor to the computer; it is and always will be complementary.

You read the two devices in different ways:

"Information [on a computer] is presented to us in a non-linear way, through an exponential series of lateral associations. The internet is a public 'space' which you visit, and even inhabit; its product is inherently impersonal and disembodied.

Scrolling documents is the opposite of reading: your eyes remain static, while the material flows past. Despite all the opportunities to 'interact', we read material from the internet…entirely passively because all the interesting associative thinking has already been done on our behalf.

Electronic media are intrinsically ephemeral, and open to perpetual revision, and work quite strenuously against any sort of historical perspective. The opposite of edited, the material on the internet is unmediated, except by the technology itself. And having no price, it has questionable value.

Finally, you can't write comments in the margin of your screen to be discovered by another reader fifty years down the line."

Lynne Truss, *Eats, Shoots and Leaves*

It speaks volumes, if you will pardon the cliché and the pun, that one of the biggest success stories on the internet is the multinational book retailer, Amazon. The blog may be in the ascendancy but blog-writers draw much of their inspiration from paper-age books which are still bought in huge numbers as carriers of ideas that are better exposed at length, in print, than as scrollable, clickable mouthfuls on screen.

As a final note on the bright future of the book, it's worth noting that the technology of print-on-demand (whereby a book exists in digital form and is only printed and bound when someone orders a copy) has now enabled the utter democratisation of the publishing process: anyone can become an author and, like the sandwich, the book has now become a receptacle for any and every ingredient imaginable. You can set up a website, but it's not the same as having physical objects in existence that you can give to people to hold in their hands.

There is a certain power in by-passing the servers of the world and committing thoughts to paper which can't be eradicated by an electro-magnetic pulse or rendered inaccessible by a power cut. The book may have begun as a medieval way of propagating the Bible but essentially it is the same information delivery system as it always was and one of its functions is still to seed subversion. As Tim Radford put it in *The Guardian*: "The invention of printing turned the book into a kind of multiple-targeted warhead: burn as many books as you like, one will always get through."

Boredom, *the end of*

In recent years, technology has achieved the near-impossible and eradicated boredom in adolescence. A mobile phone incorporating a camera, an MP3 player, a portable DVD player and a Game Boy are the complete survival kit for those daunting periods when a teenager is forced to turn off his 24-hour, multi-channel television, is banned from Facebook or has to endure a long car journey with no one but his parents for company, which means with no one.

With preparation, and as long as the batteries stay charged, an entire comfort zone can be created in pre-pubescence and carried through an entire life, without the wearer ever having to talk to an adult.

Never again will there be such a thing as downtime; never again the need to sit staring blankly at some marvelous sunset; never the need to listen to an aunty or a stranger on a train who might just have something surprising and interesting to say.

For parents, this can only be good news. Isn't this what we have always wanted from our kids – that they make their own entertainment? So what if they never learn patience, ingenuity, creativity, gratification-delay, introspection and the art of paying attention to one thing at one time – as long as they're occupied and not moaning, and leave us to play our own games in peace?

Candide

The most famous optimist in fiction is Voltaire's *Candide* (1759), a young man who is educated by his tutor Pangloss (parodying Leibniz) to believe that we live "in the best of all possible worlds" and that "everything is for the best".

Candide is chased out of the "most beautiful and most agreeable of all possible castles" by his guardian because of a misdemeanour and plunges into the barbarous outside world where he either experiences or witnesses first hand an almost complete catalogue of the misfortunes of the age including pillage, rape, murder, massacre, cannibalism, shipwreck, torture, disease, an auto-da-fé* and an earthquake.

Where we have 9/11 as the event which shattered our complacency, the 18th century had the Lisbon earthquake on All Saints' Day 1755 which killed at least 20,000 people and which forms a scene in the book. All the while, Candide tries to believe that none of these experiences by itself can invalidate Pangloss's philosophy: but he finds it hard to square each "partial evil" with the overall good of the universe and he gradually forms his own interpretation of reality.

On a superficial level, Candide can be read as a straightforward satire of Leibnizian optimism but it is more than that. Voltaire, the great defender of rationalism, uses his fable to criticise all watertight

---

*a religious ceremony including a procession, mass and sermon preceding the hanging or burning of heretics judged guilty by the Spanish Inquisition

systems of thought. The world is too rich and complex to be reduced to any formula, he is saying, and each of us must make up our own mind about any conclusions to be drawn.

Curiously, a book which is usually thought of as a methodological demolition of optimism comes to an optimistic conclusion. Candide's story is not just one of horrors but also one of kindnesses, small acts of bravery and heroism, and of humane deeds shining through grim inhumanities. Candide learns from the world and is not corrupted by it; he does not try to opt out of involvement in reality, or to console himself with cynicism, negativity or egotism. The end of the story implies that the only worthwhile response to experience, however chaotic and senseless it may be, is to learn what we can from it and make ourselves better people.

"Let's get down to work and stop all this philosophising" says Candide's companion, the everyman Martin. "It's the only way to make life bearable."

"Yes," agrees Candide, "but we must cultivate our garden."

Capital punishment

There's no easy answer to the question of what a civilised society should do with those who act in uncivilised ways. The temptation to put them to death may be a primal human response – in theory, it delivers vengeance and removes evil from the world – but killing convicted criminals, however unspeakable their crimes, is not a just solution.

The death penalty is not a matter of debatable ethics or political opinion: it is simply wrong. It runs flatly against any moral system which promotes the sanctity of human life, which includes Christianity, and is incompatible with the concept of human rights.

Neither does it make any logical sense. Pragmatic defenders of it say that it sets an example to weak-minded people and strikes fear into those dithering between right and wrong. The evidence is clear on this: the death penalty does not deter anyone from committing a crime; certainly not the man who is too screwed up or drugged, or just too young, to think about the consequences of what he is doing; and least of all the psychopath on a mass-murdering spree for whom the stakes of being caught are part of the sick game.

> "The number of countries which still have capital punishment is falling each year."

The death penalty runs contrary to the evolution of law in the modern sense. Legal systems in the western world are based on the concept of fixed-term punishments not open-ended, eternal sentences – which is what execution amounts to. Justice in the modern sense is predicated on the notion that everyone is capable of atoning for his actions and of reformation.

So, forget ethics. Forget justice being seen to be done. The only rationale for the death penalty is revenge which is a simplistic, bestial urge which should have no place in society. The state would not tolerate the family of a murder victim committing murder to balance the score, so how can it justify contracting its own hit man to do the job?

Any country (or state within the USA) that retains the death penalty does so at the expense of its own moral legitimacy. And it sets a dangerous precedent to other countries which may not have the slightest interest in the legal or moral aspects of the debate, but which may choose to execute their political prisoners on the same dubious principles.

If there are no good reasons for retaining the death penalty there is one good one for scrapping it: there are several proven examples of innocent people being executed and if this is done in the name of a state it is done in the name of every person in that state.

"If you are for the death penalty you have to say we are going to lose innocent lives but it is worth it."

Richard Dieter, director of the Death Penalty Information Center in Washington DC

The diminution of states offering the death penalty as part of their judicial menus is, therefore, directly correlated to the growth of our humanity. And the number of countries which still have capital punishment is falling each year as rational arguments outweigh passion, and constitutions are rewritten accordingly.

There will always be proponents of the death penalty as there will always be a crowd who would like to go along to the Place de la Concorde to watch blood flow, but we must never allow our passion for revenge and spectacle to overwhelm our humanity.

If you don't accept this reasoning you must ask yourself why the statistics lead in one unambiguous direction. In 1977, only 16 countries had abolished the death penalty completely; now, 90 countries do not have it, 10 retain it for crimes of an exceptional nature, and 30 have effectively if not technically abolished it. That makes 130 countries that have found other solutions for punishing serious crimes against 67 countries which still execute people. Almost all of these retentionist countries are in Africa and Asia.

The glaring exception to the trend of progress in the western world is the USA, self-proclaimed beacon of democracy and civilisation, where 38 states retain the right to stage semi-public executions: death before an invited audience. Although the macabre, Frankenstein theatricality of the electric chair is ceding to the less stressful lethal injection, this 'improvement' raises a problem. How can any doctor administer a fatal dose of a drug without violating his ethical commitment as a doctor to save life, not to deliberately take it? If the supply of Dr Deaths dries up, so will availability of the death penalty to avenging judges and governors.

Ironically, the more humane you try to make execution, the more sensibilities are raised. In 2006 there was a 'botched death' scare in the USA when a condemned man in Florida took twice as long to die (34 minutes) as normal and had chemical burns on his arms as the drugs were wrongly injected into his flesh instead of his bloodstream. Several states suspended executions in reaction and the case for abolition was strengthened.

In 2007, the surgeon Atul Gawande carried out an *ad hoc* survey of doctors in the USA for his book *Better: A Surgeon's Notes on Performance* and found that a surprising minority did not realise that involvement in an execution is an ethical issue. But Gawande points out that increasingly doctors are refusing to take part in administrative murder and predicts that the death penalty will fade away because of this.

Sources

Amnesty International: www.amnesty.org/deathpenalty

Capitalism, *caring*

Those of us near the bottom or in the middle of the income scale get the impression that those at the top are vain, smug, heartless beasts who think only about themselves. Some of them probably answer this description but not all, and although I wouldn't want to spend much of my time defending the super-rich, I'd like to spare a thought in this book for those who, often through no fault of their own, happen to be better off than ourselves.

I'd have headed this entry 'philanthropy' but I've never liked the implication that only those who are well-off can love their fellow man. And there's something very patronising, very unsocialist (with a small 'S'), about a few individuals deciding who gets how much.

Nevertheless, it is philanthropy we are talking about: people who have cash to spare and who give it away. This introduces a necessary corrective to the capitalist system which is motivated by individualism, if not selfishness.

If wealth has a way of accumulating in a few hands it is only because money is the measure of success in business. The wisest businessmen and women know that you can have enough and more than enough, and that you can only spend so much. Jim Manzi, one of the creators of the Lotus spreadsheet, said, "With $5 million you do what the hell you like. With $50 million you can do what the hell you want in a jet." According to another modern millionaire, $10 million is enough to get by on these days.

If there are almost 1000 billionaires on earth (up from 140 in 1986, according to *Forbes Magazine*, which doesn't even bother to count the millionaires) that amounts to a lot of money either to be given away or to be left uselessly in private bank accounts. Fortunately at least some of this cash is controlled by people with social consciousnesses who devote as much time to giving away money as they do to accumulating it. It doesn't really matter *why* the rich give their money away – it may be out of vanity or the search for status or the need to leave a legacy; all that matters is that they *are* giving it away. And it follows that if you want to change the world but you don't personally have the funds you can still do your bit by sitting next to the right person at dinner. One conversation can be worth a year of campaigning.

If you happen to be very rich yourself you might want to add up what you are really going to need for you and your dependents (you don't want to spoil your children by leaving them too much) over the next few decades and relish the process of handing out bundles of cash in brown envelopes to whoever you think will make best use of it. As you do, reflect on the words of the steel magnate Andrew Carnegie: "The man who dies rich dies disgraced".

Sources

Institute for Philanthropy:
www.instituteforphilanthropy.org.uk
The Network for Social Change:
thenetworkforsocialchange.org.uk

Childhood

Too many kids these days are spoiled but then again too many aren't. While some grow obese in Europe and America, almost 211 million of them in other parts of the world are obliged to work for a living, often in conditions of near slavery. And hunger remains the main challenge for many of the world's children to overcome.

But we shouldn't lose sight of the huge advances that have been made in understanding and valuing childhood. The main change that has occurred within the last hundred years in every developed country (and which we can expect to see extended to every developing country) is that cash now flows from parents to children rather than vice versa. Children have been released from production and let loose in playgrounds. Their status has simultaneously risen and they have acquired political and social rights. They are increasingly recognized as people and childhood is seen not just as a pre-adult waiting room but as an essential time of personality formation.

> *"Cash now flows from parents to children rather than vice versa."*

We should be encouraged that, in some places and in some families at least, children are respected and consulted (they have a surprising amount to say about their lives when you ask them and listen to the answers); and that charities exist to attend to the particular needs of children which are never the same as the needs of adults. The concept of

ChildLine – a phone line which children can contact without fear that the adult world will threaten or belittle them – is nothing short of enlightened.

And there are many ways in which society generally tries to make childhood more pleasant. David Bodanis describes one example of the interests of children and adults coinciding:

> "The Evelina hospital is the first new children's hospital that's been built in London in a century. There's a giant atrium in the middle, and the contract with the company doing the cleaning says that the window cleaners need to dress up as superheroes. The children in bed – many with grave illnesses – delight in seeing Superman and Spiderman dangling just inches away from them, on the outside of the glass; apparently for the cleaners it's one of the best parts of their week.
>
> The government has wasted a fortune on consultants, bureaucracy and reorganizations of the NHS. It's always defended in cold management-speak. This simple arrangement with the window cleaners cuts through all that."

Clarke's guide to the impossible

In *Profiles of the Future: An Inquiry into the Limits of the Possible,* Arthur C. Clarke set down the first of his laws and, almost as an afterthought, a comment which his French publisher interpreted as a second law. In response, Clarke added a third law.

Clarke's First Law

"When a distinguished but elderly scientist states that something is possible, he is almost certainly right. When he states that something is impossible, he is very probably wrong. Perhaps the adjective 'elderly' requires definition. In physics, mathematics and astronautics it means over thirty; in other disciplines, senile decay is sometimes postponed to the forties. There are, of course, glorious exceptions; but as every researcher just out of college knows, scientists of over fifty are good for nothing but board meetings, and should at all costs be kept out of the laboratory."

Clarke's Second Law

"The only way of discovering the limits of the possible is to venture a little way past them into the impossible."

Clarke's Third Law

"Any sufficiently advanced technology is indistinguishable from magic."

Climate change *(for believers)*

"The environmental problems are much too serious to be left to the pessimists... We must awaken the enlightening spirit of reinventing everything, the future included. Pessimism is a self-falsifying prophecy. Optimism always wins. Until nobody is around to know that it did not."

Tor Nørretranders, author of 'The Generous Man'

The apocalyptic obsession of the moment, need you be reminded, is that we humans are gradually and inexorably fouling our own nest, like so many chain smokers shut in a closed room chanting "I'll quit if you will" to each other as the last particles of oxygen are used up.

Listen to some experts – and this is a field in which pundits proliferate – and you could get the impression that there is nothing we can do about climate change except wait for it to visit its violence on us as a cosmic I Told You So. Writing in the *Daily Telegraph*, the journalist Tom Fort wondered aloud whether the end of the world may not be preferable to hearing endless prophecies about it.

The first and most popular way of being optimistic about ice caps melting, sea levels rising, freak storms prowling the earth and the Gulf Stream running cold is to deny that any of these things are happening or ever going to happen. In our black-and-white world, we divide into believers of the doomsday scenario and 'climate change deniers' (qv), who are willing to risk being ostracized by the believers for their alternative theorising. Most climate change 'believers', it should be said, are adamant that the 'deniers' have no viable case to make given the evidence available.

If we accept that climate change is happening, we still don't have to despair. Human ingenuity should be capabe of providing a solution. After all, if we can produce mobile phones for every teenager in Europe, surely we can convert our economy to run on non-polluting energy sources and help developing countries (particularly India and China) to enjoy lifestyles on a par with ours without repeating our environmental mistakes.

Mark Lynas, author of *High Tide* and *Six Degrees*, who once confronted the 'climate change sceptic' Bjorn Lomborg with a custard pie, is adamant that changing our lifestyles is not the same thing as becoming ascetics. In his view, we can actually improve the quality of our lives:

> "...a future where we use less energy, where we generate it cleanly and where we use it more sensibly, is going to be a future where most of us will live richer, more fulfilled lives than ever before."

We can now design houses that need virtually no heating. Energy can be generated by small scale plants which means its production can be democratised. The only thing we really have to give up, says Lynas, is 'binge' flying. For continental journeys, we can take the train but long-haul trips are not environmentally defensible.

According to Jeffrey Sachs, the 2007 BBC Reith lecturer, we'll solve this environmental crisis as we solved the last one, the hole in the ozone layer (remember that?). From crisis to resolution took four stages:

i. Denials by the polluters – "As soon as the science came, came the companies with the vested interests claiming junk science, because their instinct is to start lobbying. But you don't lobby against nature. Nature has its principles: it doesn't matter what the boards of these companies say. What matters is the actual physical mechanisms. The science was right, it becomes more and more known."

⇩

ii. NASA took a photograph of the hole in the ozone layer from space and this indisputable visual evidence . . .

⇩

iii. turned public opinion in favour of doing something about the problem, and consumers and voters put pressure on . . .

⇩

iv. the polluting companies who realised they could solve the problem, and in the 1990s a framework was established to stop the use of CFCs (the gases which were depleting the ozone layer).

The process of change took 15 years. The same could happen with climate change.

> "The good news is that the scientists and the engineers are now scurrying. Technological alternatives are being developed. Carbon capture and sequestration is beginning to be put into place in demonstration projects. So too are alternative non-fossil fuel energy sources, and so too remarkable breakthroughs in energy efficiency, such as hybrid and plug-in hybrid automobiles, which promise us vast efficiency gains, more distance per unit of fuel.
>
> The good news is that those technological breakthroughs are similarly leading the companies to whisper in the ears of the politicians - 'it's okay, we can handle this.' And that's the best news of all. Companies around the world are now in the lead of their politicians. In fact they're telling the politicians we have to act, we want a framework, we need an incentive mechanism, we need a price structure so that we can move ahead with sustainable energy.
>
> We will learn that the costs of action are tiny, compared with the risks of inaction. Climate change can be solved, according to the best current estimates, for less than one per cent of world income each year, and perhaps well under that, where the potential costs are a devastating multiple of several per cent of world income if we continue on the business-as-usual trajectory."

Jeffrey Sachs, Reith Lecture 2007

Climate change *(for deniers)*

Environmental sceptics offer three rebuttals to the principal climate change arguments. Theirs is an optimistic outlook which doesn't require anyone to make drastic sacrifices or to suffer:

1. **Scientific rebuttal**

   Humanity isn't having as much impact on the environment as campaigners 'like' to claim. The earth has natural climatic cycles which are far beyond our control; weather patterns are also affected by sunspots, which again have nothing to do with how many flights people take. There are, the sceptics say, always doomsday prophecies being proclaimed; now it's global warming but not so long ago it was global cooling.

2. **Moral rebuttal**

   The proposed costs of dealing with climate change will fall on the poorest nations and the poorest people in the world. It is not justifiable to ask developing countries to accept less comfortable, less polluting standards of living than people in the west have enjoyed for decades.

3. **Economic rebuttal**

   The costs of dealing with climate change in the way proposed will be exorbitant – it will be cheaper to adapt to the effects of climate change as and when they occur, than to try to avert them. The best way to deal with the situation is not do anything, that is, not to interfere. We need to let the free market sort things out. If renewable energies, for example, can be shown to be profitable, people will switch to using them.

Much of the debate is to do with how far our style of living is sustainable, or whether we can continue to enjoy economic growth and still hope to save the climate. The sceptics argue that resources are not finite and cannot, according to orthodox market theory, be depleted at an unsustainable rate because as supply falls so prices rise and demand is reduced. Technological improvements also make for the more efficient use of resources and effectively increase supply.

The late economist Julian Simon graphically and conclusively demonstrated that this was not just theory when he challenged the environmentalist Paul Ehrlich to take a bet in 1980. Ehrich maintained that one day the earth would no longer be able to meet the demands of humanity. Simon bet him that any trend of material human welfare would improve in any country over any time scale over ten years. Ehrlich took expert advice and nominated five metals whose value he was sure could only go up: copper, chrome, nickel, tin and tungsten. In 1990, on the day nominated in the bet, all the metals had declined in price and Ehrlich was forced to concede defeat and send a cheque to Simon. The price had gone down because of technological progress, said Simon: either more efficient mining methods had been developed or synthetic alternatives had been invented.

Simon's dictum works just as well, he declared, for a

basic commodity such as food: "the fact is that whatever the rate of population growth happens to be, the rate of the food supply tends to increase even faster," resulting in obesity in some countries rather than scarcity. *Ergo*, to cope with climate change, if it is really occurring, all we need to do, Simon concluded, is allow technology and free trade to grow unimpeded.

Simon distinguished between 'builders' and 'stoppers' in all walks of life and accused strident environmentalists of being the latter, wanting to interfere, regulate and artificially engineer solutions. "Environmentalism is a luxury good," he declared "something you can afford but don't need."

> "If a man is a pessimist he wears a belt as well as braces; if he is an optimist he wears neither."
> Lord Dewar 1924

Colour

A 32-bit digital image deploys billions of colours in its efforts to render reality on a computer screen, and a 48-bit image offers trillions. The human eye can only discern about 10 million different colours, so most of these colours are superfluous but it's nice to know they're there.

We live in a world quite literally saturated with colour and you could say the world is getting ever brighter. We've come a long way from Bronze Age dyeing when a few plants were used to make murky, non-colour fast hues. The invention of synthetic dyes in the 19th century changed everything and led the way for cheap, mass market gaudy fabrics, paints and home furnishings.

Whereas in the Middle Ages, only emperors could afford to paint their bedrooms in purple because there just weren't enough shellfish to supply everyone, now you can paint your windows and your children purple, dye your hair purple and eat purple food if the mood takes you.

Further thought

The Society of Dyers and Colourists: www.sdc.org.uk and www.colour-experience.org

Community

More people now inhabit virtual worlds on the internet such as Second Life than live in Australia. You can only wonder which way these people would jump if they had to choose between life in the outback with its flies and rotting kangaroo carcasses or 'life' without blemish in a simulated universe circumscribed by a 17-inch computer screen.

Of course, there is no reason why you shouldn't live on a sheep station in the Northern Territory *and* move an avatar (your online personality) around cybersuburbia during your spare time, which is what people do. Despite all the temptations to please ourselves and isolate ourselves from the world, community (in the real sense) is doing pretty well.

In an important way, we're not fully human when we're not part of a community. You can build a log cabin in the woods and dress yourself in rabbit skins but it won't take you far down the road towards civilisation. You'll have to spend most of your time gathering food and you probably won't be able to scrape together a full opera company from the surrounding hills. You certainly won't have a broadband connection.

Life in a community undoubtedly showers us with benefits but it demands sacrifices and that's why the internet is so appealing: you log on and log off when you want. In real life you wake up and you have to be your avatar all day long, whatever you feel like.

Communities (of the real, physical variety) serve important functions, in particular giving protection to the very young and very old and a sense of belonging to everyone. Clearly, the online community looks after no one's granny so we should be careful not to lose sight of the real meaning of the word.

But it does seem as if we can be part of many different communities at the same time and perhaps we can have the best of all communal worlds. As well as the communities that we are born into and live in there are communities we find ourselves a part of by comradeship – minorities surrounded by an semi-inhospitable culture, such as the gay community or the 'trans' community (those not happy with the gender of their birth). Then there are elective communities: societies, pressure groups, political parties and so on.

Some people leave the communities of their origins to join model communities – utopian (in the good sense of the word) or New Age (not that this means much) – which are striving for new ways of assembly. Two examples of communities of the new kind are Findhorn, in Scotland, which grew up on the sand-dunes beside a beautiful tidal bay as a spiritual community (without fixed creed) and Damanhur in Italy, a mini-society based on optimism but also on business acumen, which has its own flag and currency. Neither is perfect – which community, old or new, is? – but both are attempts to put ways of living together to the test and the results can be usefully applied in other contexts. Such places can be thought of as serving four functions at the same time: they are living experiments; they educate visitors; they act as hubs for many interlocking networks; and they transmit new ideas to the world.

William James visited a utopian community at Lake Chautauqua in the late 19th century, "a foretaste of what human society might be, were it all in the light, with no suffering and no dark corners." But his reaction on leaving it surprised him:

"And yet what was my own astonishment, on emerging into the dark and wicked world again, to catch myself quite unexpectedly and involuntarily saying: 'Ouf! what a relief!' Now for something primordial and savage, even though it were as bad as an Armenian massacre, to set the balance straight again. This order is too tame, this culture too second-rate, this goodness too uninspiring. This human drama without a villain or a pang; this community so refined that ice-cream soda-water is the utmost offering it can make to the brute animal in man; this city simmering in the tepid lakeside sun; this atrocious harmlessness of all things, I cannot abide with them. Let me take my chances again in the big outside worldly wilderness with all its sins and sufferings. There are the heights and depths, the precipices and the steep ideals, the gleams of the awful and the infinite; and there is more hope and help a thousand times than in this dead level and quintessence of every mediocrity."

What was lacking was:

> "the element of precipitousness, so to call it, of strength and strenuousness, intensity and danger… the everlasting battle of the powers of light with those of darkness… there was no potentiality of death in sight anywhere, and no point of the compass visible from which danger might possibly appear… The moment the fruits are being merely eaten, things become ignoble."

Surprisingly perhaps, virtual communities are not perfect either. Everything bad from the real world seeps down cables into what was once virgin electronic territory. Crime, pornography and other evils lurk in 'second lives'. Technology puts you in control but only to an extent. You can log off when you want and that is what differentiates the virtual world from the world of commitment to people who might bang on your door asking for help at antisocial hours. When you meet people virtually, all your interactions are virtual.

There again, virtual communities offer some advantages to some people that real communities do not. Paralysed people with cerebral palsy are able to go online and make such untranscendental decisions about what clothes to wear and they can also experience what it means to fly.

Far better is for us to maintain existing communities if we can and adapt them to meet the demands for greater personal freedom. To some extent we are learning to do this and it is encouraging that for all the consumerism and individualism rampant in the world, there are communities that manage to cling together. Most of the world's economic migrants do not travel solely in search of an improvement in their own material lot but to send back money to their families. If we're wise, which we are when we're not being mesmerised by shining objects like the internet, we'll remember that life is not worth much if we live it alone. Does anyone really aspire to be a billionaire, isolated in a mini-paradise of his own creation behind 8-foot high security fences? Don't answer that.

Sources

Findhorn: www.findhorn.org
Damanhur: www.damanhur.org

Conspiracy theories

Evidence and proof are dull commodities which can stunt the imagination. They may make reliable science and trustworthy law enforcement but they reduce history to the pedestrian preserve of people who know what they are talking about.

What most of us prefer is the mischievous feeling that the experts could be wrong. Which is why it is comforting to know that there are still some mystery stories from recent history to be solved. If every event was a watertight case of cause and effect what would there be to look forward to?

From time to time, someone pops up with the clinching 'evidence' to prove a conspiracy theory unfounded; but we know it's just another expert earning his living and that he's almost certainly part of the conspiracy he repudiates.

If we stick around long enough, all will be revealed and our curiosity will be satisfied. Sooner or later a vault will be opened or an attic cleaned out and papers will turn up proving that Marilyn Monroe, Princess Di and Pope John Paul I were murdered, and that JFK wasn't assassinated by a lone killer.

Whatever we're told or shown, we still won't believe the official version. Especially if the truth turns out to be mundane: murder because of mistaken identity or petty motive; cover-up by cock-up; or evidence destroyed by the bureaucratic indecision of a bunch of incompetents.

Courage

At the time of writing Aung San Suu Kyi is still campaigning for democracy for Myanmar (formerly Burma), having spent much of the last twenty years under house arrest or forbidden to return to Burma if she leaves the country. She has had to endure long periods of separation from her family in Britain to do what she sees as her duty to her country and to the memory of her father (assassinated in 1947, when she was two years old) who played a pivotal role in Burma's independence. She barely saw her children grow up and was not able to be with her husband when he died in 1999.

Worse than the actual separation is the capital the authorities in Myanmar have made of it, trying to portray her as a glory-seeker who is willing to neglect her children for the sake of her political ambitions.

Fame and the Nobel Peace Prize have given her a high profile in the world but we should not forget that there are other less well-known campaigners and prisoners of conscience who behave with similar fortitude and it is such stubborn people who drive good forward in the world. Among these people are many journalists who risk their lives in order to make sure that stories that should be told are told. Many journalists die each year, simply for asking too many questions of authority.

In his recent book *Courage*, the British prime minister Gordon Brown concludes that not all courage is the kind seen on a battlefield, the risk of injury or danger: there is also "courage that comes from cultivating the habit of refusing to let fear dictate one's actions, courage that could be described as 'grace under pressure'." It is not an innate or instinctive response, it is not calculated; it can only be tested in action. And courage, as Nelson Mandela, points out in his autobiographies multiplies when it is shared.

> *"An optimist is a man who starts a crossword puzzle with a fountain pen."*
>
> Anon

Death

Find something positive to say about death – there's a challenge for any optimist. What else can we do but square up to the inevitable: it's coming, so you may as well prepare yourself and handle it as well as you can (known as "having a good death"). You could even arrange for it to happen at the time of your own choosing (don't say suicide, say voluntary euthanasia). If you're lucky it will spring at you unawares and you'll never know anything about it.

If you wonder why we die at all (see 'Immortality') you should reflect for a moment on what would happen if the earth simply accumulated individual human beings without letting them go. You should also consider what it would do to our psychology if death were removed from the world. Knowing that we are not here forever gives an impulse to our actions and a poignancy to our lives, from which derives our sense of beauty and wonder in the deepest sense.

> *"I do not fear death, in view of the fact that I had been dead for billions and billions of years before I was born, and had not suffered the slightest inconvenience from it."*
>
> Mark Twain

If what keeps you awake at night is not how you are going to die but what happens afterwards, you've got nothing to worry about either. The empirical evidence is – to put it crudely – that consciousness shuts down like a computer when the power cord is yanked from the wall, leaving only a big bag of useless cells which barely wait for you to vacate the premises before they pack and go their separate ways, the servants dismissed after a lifetime's service in the big house. That, at least, is how it looks from the outside.

From the inside we simply don't know what happens and that should be a source of reassurance. Whatever science says, it is hard to believe that we are no more than the sum of our tangible components; that this sensation of 'I-ness' which we ascribe to the mind simply fades to nought. Supposedly, 22 grams of us evaporate at the moment of death and this is said to be the weight of the soul but you'd have to have some religious faith to derive any hope from this.

Even if something survives – the soul, the mind – it's almost certain that you will leave behind your personality and memory which can be assumed to be formed by the interaction of your genes with the environment over the course of your lifetime and stored in your biodegradable brain.

It could be that consciousness is recycled when the body and the personality die. The philosopher and interpreter of eastern thought Alan Watts gave an elegant explanation of this:

> "When I am dead I will be in the same state I was before I was born, and it will be as if I never had been born. Before I was born there was a world, there were things going on. If I go back when I'm dead to the state I was in before I was born,

couldn't I happen again? The body comes out of the universe. It is the universe which is living in the same way a tree produces apples. It seems absolutely reasonable to assume that when I die and this physical body evaporates and the whole memory system with it, then the awareness that I had before will begin all over once again."

You might reoccur as a fruit fly or worm, of course, but you can worry about that when the time comes. The important thing is to live now without fearing death.

"There's nothing in that nothing to be afraid of. With that sense you can come on like the rest of your life is gravy because you're already dead: You know you are going to die. Regard yourself as dead already so that you have nothing to lose. A Turkish proverb says, 'he who sleeps on the floor will not fall out of bed.'"

"The more you know you are nothing the more you will amount to something."

Whatever happens afterwards, you can be sure that you'll only have to live death once and it will immediately cancel out all the pain of living and the pain of dying.

Sources

Death, by Alan Watts (1975)
Heaven: A Traveller's Guide to the Undiscovered Country, by Peter Stanford (2002)

Democracy

Democracy is a simple but strange idea which is difficult to put into practice in anything but an imperfect form. It was first applied in 5th century BC Greece by a politician named Cleisthenes, although a more colourful theory says that it began as a system of decision making among trireme oarsmen who used it to agree their objectives and conditions of service.

Either way, it's a big leap from 60 men engaged in life or death naval manoeuvres, or 6,000 citizens (excluding women and slaves) attending an open-air assembly in Athens, to a modern country of 60 million (or even 1 billion) people organised into a fully-functioning state. It's a mad, bold notion that everyone over 18, absolutely everyone, should be consulted about the composition of the government and we're still trying to figure out how to determine the will of the majority accurately. With so many people and such varieties of education, living standards and political awareness, how can you determine the majority view on anything minor let alone everything major that must be done? All our democracies are really democracies in evolution and we should quietly admit that democracy is really only a fancy name for responsible oligarchy, rule by an appointed elite.

However, the essential two differences between dictatorship and democracy are that governments can and do change and that the clunking, bureaucratic machinery of the system is, as far as possible, exposed to press and public scrutiny.

Fundamentally, the really great advantage of living in a democracy is not having the right to vote but knowing that you are subject to a rule of law which rests on the assumption of every citizen being equal in power to every other, however inarticulate or vulnerable. This principle grants freedom of action and speech to all, freedoms which are enforced by the judiciary and the police.

That such ideas are still revolutionary in many parts of the world is a good reason for us to peddle democracy as the best political system we can think of for now, but we should be wary of trying to impose our variation of it on anyone else.

Sources

The Aquarian Conspiracy, by Marilyn Ferguson (1980)

In Defence of Politics, by Bernard Crick (1962)

Dentists

Even if your mother couldn't make you brush your teeth regularly with her bribes and threats, when your molars start to work loose, or crack from decades of neglect, you will be able to sit in a modern dental surgery where you will be treated by a competent professional to whom hygiene and customer satisfaction are priorities, and who is highly motivated by the thought of his/her next skiing holiday.

Look at any museum of dental implements – and which of us doesn't head straight for the nearest whenever we're visiting a new town? – and you will remind yourself that the angst of modern living is more than compensated for by not having to ask the local barber to deal with your toothache.

"The sky is no less blue because the clouds obscure it or because the blind cannot see it."
Danish proverb

Diamond, *John*

Three months before his death in March 2001, at the age of 47, the British journalist John Diamond was set a peculiar brief by *The Observer*:

> "This was the first commission I've had in 20-odd years in the game which read quite so much like an extract from a suicide note. 'Just tell me, John, what the hell is the point of it all?' "

The result was an article of tentative and poignant optimism, 'Reasons to be Cheerful'.

To set the context, Diamond explains that he is suffering from "an apparently terminal illness". It takes an optimist to insert the word 'apparently' in this sentence as by this stage of his illness his tongue had been removed, he was suffering from "a fair to middling amount of pain on most days" and the prognostic was that he might only have two months left to live.

The article continues:

> "It's a fair assumption on the part of my inquisitors: with so little time left for living, what is there to live for? The easy answer is Philip Larkin's about none of us ever being able to get out of bed in the morning if we had any real sense of our own mortality."

And then John Diamond provides his own answer to the question 'what is there to live for?'

"We have a limited capacity for happiness, but an almost infinitely unlimited capacity for, well, not unhappiness exactly, but non-happiness... This is what it's all about. It's about reading a paper on a Sunday morning while you're thinking about whether you can be arsed to go to the neighbours' New Year's Eve party tonight. It's about getting angry with me for having different opinions from yours or not expressing the ones you have as well as you would have expressed them. It's about the breakfast you've just had and the dinner you're going to have. It's about the random acts of kindness which still, magically, preponderate over acts of incivility or nastiness. It's about rereading *Great Expectations* and about who's going to win the 3.30 at Haydock Park. It's about being able to watch old episodes of Frasier on satellite TV whenever we want, having the choice of three dozen breakfast cereals and seven brands of virgin olive oil at Sainsbury's. It's about loving and being loved, about doing the right thing, about one day being missed when we're gone....

It is, above all I suppose, about passing time.

And the simple answer to the question 'What the hell is the point of it all' is *this* is the point of it all. You aren't happy? Yes you are: this, here, now, is what happiness is. Enjoy it."

Sources

'Reasons to be Cheerful', *The Observer* on 31st December 2000

John Diamond is also the author of *C: Because Cowards Get Cancer Too...* (1999)

Disease, *eradication of*

Human beings may have clubbed to death the inoffensive dodo but they do not, thankfully, make a habit of wilful specicide. No one, however, can be sentimental about our success in driving the smallpox virus to extinction.

In the 18th century, the little beggar killed five reigning monarchs and 60 million other people. In the 20th century it claimed at least 300 million lives before war against it was declared and won, making it the first and only human infectious disease to be eradicated from nature. First it was pushed back to the Horn of Africa and the last natural case occurred in Somalia in 1977. There was one last fatal case in the United Kingdom when the disease was acquired from laboratory stock but eradication was confirmed in 1980.

Polio is next on the World Health Organisation's hit list: the number of cases is dropping; they are mainly confined to Nigeria and India; and there is a chance of seeing the back of the disease by 2010.

The next big fight after that is, or should be, against malaria which can be prevented by a combination of relatively inexpensive measures such as supplying bed nets to families in infected zones.

Sources

World Health Organization: www.who.int

Economics, *new thinking in*

If globalisation is what happens when heartless, dinosaurian corporations stalk the planet unchallenged and unchecked – which is one definition – we might want to look closer to the ground for signs of incipient life ready to evolve into something more intelligent, sensitive and sustainable. The reptilian global city may have become one big shopping centre full of the same few chain stores selling the same small selection of bland brand goods but in the global village small-scale enterprise is experimenting with diversified, decentralised economic models for the future.

In the developed world, there are two interesting phenomena to note, the local and the virtual. Going back to the basis of what business is all about, several communities have organised themselves into Local Employment and Trading Systems or 'Lets', a sophisticated version of bartering using pretend units of currency with colourful names that people can relate to (*Bobbins* in Manchester, *Bricks* in Brixton, *Readies* in Reading and *Olivers* in Bath) which allows people within a defined area to trade skills and resources without 'real' money changing hands. Lets, so far, have only been proven to work on a small scale (the largest has just over 300 members) but exclusivity is a virtue: the currency can't be converted into anything transportable and so wealth stays locked in the Lets community. Lets probably won't ever take over the world but at least they make people think about money and trade in a new way: "…if people really catch on, local communities could wrest back some power from unaccountable banks, supermarkets, chancellors and the infernal, mysterious, supranational economic system," John Vidal explained in *The Guardian* in 1994.

An extension of the Lets is Freecycle, an internet-based way of giving away the stuff you don't need to someone who wants it. Both systems bear witness to the truth of Robert Putnam's principal of 'social capital': that networks based on trust between friends, and members of the same family or community facilitate business and hence have value even if they are not built into conventional economic calculations.

Online, meanwhile, there is a whole new world of trading and bartering which by-passes anything we can call a normal marketplace. eBay and other web-based companies which introduce a seller to a buyer who may live on the other side of the world are creating a revolutionary economic lifestyle. The internet is becoming an infinitely large bric-a-brac stall where even a niche business exploiting a highly specialised demand can make a good living without having to pay for shop premises.

Technological prophets like Kevin Kelly, author of *New Rules for the New Economy* keep telling us that we haven't fully understood that it is not just the speed but also the nature of business that is changing. Never was a name more aptly chosen than the 'web' which links all nodes and strands to each other without having to go through centralised systems. You don't have to understand anything about computers to realise that when everything becomes digitisable and hence copiable, traditional notions of ownership and copyright are bound to disappear. And the pace of change will not abate: flux will become the norm and the importance of tradition, location and opening hours will cede to 'anything, anytime, anywhere'. Some things, however, remain the same. Flexibility, attentiveness to demand and responsiveness will always be business virtues and there will always be a role for the corner shop willing to stay open long hours to supply late night munchies to cybernauts.

Other constants are sociability and solidarity which are, in the long run, inseparable from business. The internet may be making eBay millionaires but it is also putting people in rich and poor countries into contact like never before. One commendable innovation is Kiva, a website which puts would-be investors in touch with entrepreneurs in other parts of the world who need almost pathetically small amounts of cash to enable their businesses to grow.

Kiva is part of a growing economic sector called microfinance which came to world attention in 2006 when Muhammad Yunus won the Nobel Peace Prize for his work with the Grameem Bank in Bangladesh. There are estimated to be 3,000 such banks in the world providing small loans to 92 million borrowers among the world's poorest people – the vast majority of them women. The idea is that a tiny amount of money (typically less than $100) can make an enormous difference to a would-be entrepreneur and that if an economy is given a push to get going it will eventually look after itself. The concept of microfinance has been criticized for being merely a new way to distribute gifts and subsidies from the rich world, and a way of buoying up the poor-with-means rather than the desperate poor, but essentially no one can deny that the means to start or expand a business should be available to everyone.

It would be encouraging to be able to say that only socially-conscious businesses thrive but it would not be true. We can, however, say that it is possible to run a successful company *and* contribute to the local community.

> "A tiny amount of money can make an enormous difference to a would-be entrepreneur and that if an economy is given a push to get going it will eventually look after itself."

One example of a business which takes its social responsibilities seriously is Walkerswood in Jamaica, which produces jerk (barbecue) seasoning, coconut rundown sauce, Solomon gundy fish paste and rum marmalade. Although it started as a nominally colonialist venture its development was influenced by Fabianism and its family owners consider the provision of local employment and the respectful treatment of farmers to be more important than the maximisation of profits.

Even more heartwarming is Mirembe Kawomera (meaning 'Delicious Peace'), a coffee co-operative in Uganda which forms part of the Thanksgiving Coffee Co. Putting communal prosperity ahead of sectarianism, it brings together Jewish, Muslim and Christian farmers in the same enterprise.

All of which adds up to a lot of individual economic initiative at ground level all around the world and many different ways of doing business other than the vertically structured multinational with globalising tendencies and an obsession with profit over all other considerations.

Sources

Freecycle: www.freecycle.org
Kiva: www.kiva.org
New Rules for the New Economy, by Kevin Kelly (2003)
Walkerswood: www.walkerswood.com
Mirembe Kawomera: www.mirembekawomera.com

Education

Tony Blair was right when, at the start of his term as PM, he stressed the value of education. No one disputes nowadays that all children should go to school but despite more than a century of experimentation, the world has never reached agreement on what they should learn after acquiring the three Rs. There are piles of books and endless studies on the subject; it would be nice if some consensus could emerge from all that we have been learning about learning and I suspect that it will.

One thing is for sure: a free education must be extended to all children in the world. On the plus side, the number attending primary school has increased from 8/10 to 9/10 in the last 20 years – but that still leaves 100 million out of the school system. I hope also that policy in the future will focus on four areas beyond the basics:

1. Separating the learning of knowledge from religion, just as politics is becoming increasingly secularised.

2. Teaching all young children a second language: bilingualism automatically breaks down communication barriers and makes it less likely that adults fall into the trap of thinking as 'us' and 'them'.

3. Fostering creativity as a core element of the curriculum. Not just for the sake of learning to paint or make music but also to develop skills in creative thinking and problem solving

4. Nurturing a sense of self-worth, right and responsibility, including the management of emotions and an understanding of the citizen's role in democracy.

Email

Some things become so much part of life that you don't even notice them. Kids now send messages to each other through the ether by stabbing a return key. It's difficult to explain to them that when we had the urge to text a friend we first had to trek to the stationer's for paper and an envelope, then find a post office to buy a stamp, then go home to write the letter (if the urge hadn't left you by that time) and finally go out again to look for a post box. If we were lucky we'd get a reply within a week.

Those of us who remember the introduction of the fax as a piece of magic which eliminated letter writing will always marvel at the grace and simplicity of email (and texting). Not only is email an instant extension of your stream of consciousness into someone else's, a silent flow of thoughts between the two of you not far short of telepathy, but it is also wonderfully egalitarian and smoothes out all differences between people. There is no age, race or geography when you are in the world of email.

One of the greatest benefits it has delivered is to reconnect parents and grandparents with their selfish, footloose children and grandchildren. The young, who would never think of phoning home and who only answer their mobile when the ringtone tells them it is someone fun never go far without checking their messages or email inbox and are happy to write a few words back because this way they can keep the oldies satisfied but at a distance.

Energy

What we all want to hear on this subject is that we can go on living carelessly, using and squandering energy without guilt, and without eco-puritans pointing the finger.

Potentially, we have every reason to be optimistic. There is no shortage of energy in the universe to power the future and keep our lifestyles going without further polluting the planet. As Alun Anderson, a senior consultant (and former Editor-in-Chief) for the *New Scientist*, summarises the situation:

> "70 per cent of our energy needs come from burning fossil fuels but the amount of potential energy available to us is enormous: 3,000,000 x 10^20 joules. That is the amount of clean, green energy that pours down on the Earth totally free of charge every year. The Sun is providing 7,000 times as much energy as we are using, which leaves plenty for developing China, India and everyone else."

In practical terms, we need to capture all this free energy and turn it into clean, efficient, commercial power, available to everyone on earth. That's quite a challenge with one billion people not yet on the bottom rung of the energy ladder and a further three billion only just meeting their basic energy requirements.

The energy industry, however, is confident that we can adapt to future demands and meet the needs of all the world's population, not just those of people in rich countries. No one is sure exactly how we'll heat our homes by the end of the 21st century but then at the start of the 20th century, who could have foreseen today's diverse energy mix?

For now we'll have to rely on existing energy sources. There's cause for concern but not for panic. We keep hearing that the oil is about to run out but according to a 2001 Shell publication we're probably all right until 2025, possibly to 2040. It's a similar story for gas although the levels of reserves are more uncertain.

Energy efficiency will help conserve existing stocks. The same Shell booklet maintains that "efficiency could more than double simply through widespread diffusion of existing and anticipated technologies" and "various studies suggest that a fourfold, or even greater improvement in efficiency is possible."

Known or 'incumbent' energy sources will dovetail into new or 'disruptive' alternatives – i.e. forms of energy that take us by surprise and change the way we live. In 1900, it looked as if the race to perfect the automobile would be won by either steam or electric power rather than the internal combustion engine which was noisy, polluting and difficult to crank start. The car as we know it developed because Henry Ford's low-cost mass production system and consumer choice led to its widespread adoption and hence stimulated the competition which could finance rapid refinement of the technology. Similarly the winners in the race to replace oil will have to fight it out with unsuccessful technologies.

Wind and solar power could well be part of the mix but a way will have to be found to store their energy if they are to make a significant contribution. However, they might be able to trade on their decentralising, democratising credentials: if people in rural areas and blocks of flats in urban areas are able to free themselves from the grid at an affordable price, these technologies will take off. Maybe there are other surprises waiting for us such as the return of the commercial sailing boat to carry cargoes around the world at minimal cost.

Smart money at the moment is on super-efficient static or vehicle engines running on hydrogen fuel cell technology.

The truth is we don't know how we will power the future but the probability is that we will manage it with ease and worry can be a very good stimulus to action. One positive outcome from the present climate debate could be the emergence of a revolutionary fuel source. As the Shell booklet says, "real or perceived environmental crises can accelerate technological advances."

Sources

Energy Saving Trust: www.energysavingtrust.org.uk
Energy Future: www.energyfuture.org.uk
Centre for Alternative Technology: www.cat.org.uk

Europeans, *700 million not yet redundant*

No one in the rest of the world is going to shed tears when China and India leapfrog Europe to become the next economic (and political) superpowers but Europeans will still have something to contribute.

We're a rather vaguely defined continent, with not much holding us together as peoples, and we have a checkered, domineering history to live down, but we also have good points. We've experimented an awful lot during the 20th century with all sorts of marvellous and horrendous ideas, and we can quietly but confidently put ourselves forward as the world's consultants on:

- Absorbing immigrants, and giving them opportunities if not always welcoming them as much as we could.

- Political transitions (think Spain and the eastern bloc).

- Coalition democracy – not an easy trick to pull off.

- Rising from the ashes and rebuilding countries.

- Multiculturalism: allowing or encouraging and living with diversity.

- Humanitarianism and the protection of rights.

- Hanging on to tradition in the face of globalisation. We have a nice line in heritage preservation and we're pretty good at conserving other civilisations' works of art too which, one day, we may have to give back.

- Religious toleration – we've had our bad times but we've learned.

- Valuing the good things in life – art, food (ask the French).

- Transportation in areas of dense population.

- Coping with disparities between poverty and prosperity.

On the whole, we're an old, enterprising, highly adaptable culture with the best of intentions. We're like some old seadog with a craggy face, experience and a little wisdom, and lots of good stories to tell about places and times far away. We might have had our golden age, or ages, but surely we can be of service when other continents and countries get their turn?

> "I'm an optimist, but an optimist who carries a raincoat."
> Harold Wilson

Evil

In 1971 the basement of the psychology department of Stanford University was turned into a prison as an experiment in human behaviour. The idea was to watch what would happen to good (normal) people who were put into an abnormal situation. The result, as Philip Zimbardo, social psychologist, remembers it was "more like a Greek drama than an experiment".

Male student volunteers chosen for their normality were turned into pretend prisoners and guards. Everything was done to boost the power of the guards and make the prisoners feel powerless – they were, for example, forced to wear smocks without underpants. On the first day, nothing of interest happened but after that things turned nasty and the guards took advantage of their power to dehumanise and abuse those in their charge. "They were simulating sodomy in five days. At that point we had to end the study."

None of which offers any reassurance about human nature or a future without evil – events in Abu Graib prison in Iraq in 2003, for instance, proved that the experiment was an accurate representation of reality. But at least we know that when you put good people in an evil place – which may just mean giving them power and weaponry and withdrawing the senior officer – they are likely to egg each other on until they are wallowing in thrilling immorality.

"Systems create situations which corrupt individuals," concludes Zimbardo, but the system always blames the individuals – a few bad apples – and gets itself off the moral hook. To say this is not to place all the blame on the anonymous system and to exonerate the individuals with the cell keys, guns and digital cameras; we are each responsible for our behaviour, whatever uniform we wear, whatever hierarchy we form a part of; whatever orders we are given. And it is not to say that systems do not themselves sometimes act with decisive evil and spin an extraordinary logic of their own to justify themselves. "No-one in history ever said, 'I'm doing evil'. It's 'I'm doing good'." Usually people do institutional evil in the furtherance of 'national security'. As long as there is an enemy, with or without a name and country (nowadays 'terrorism' is enough of a label) there will be someone who thinks he is wearing shining armour as he flies a flight of extraordinary rendition to some amoral participating state where torture is justified so that the rest of us may sleep safe in our beds.

> "No one in history ever said 'I'm doing evil'. It's 'I'm doing good'."

If we want to prevent evil, we must first acknowledge that all of us – including you and me – are capable of it if we're placed in circumstances that permit it to flourish. By recognizing the inevitability of evil we can prevent it, by using our votes and our voices against politicians and systems that through malice or negligence, allow these circumstances to be created.

There is, however, a straightforward piece of optimism to end this cautionary tale. In evil circumstances a few individuals do not behave badly; they do not turn a blind eye but actively challenge their abusive comrades and the system itself. Zimbardo calls these people true heroes: the kind of people who possess the qualities that most of us do not. These ordinary people who show extraordinary courage could be role models for society and their attitudes could be taught to the young. To understand the preconditions for evil and to anticipate it by teaching people to think for themselves and act with honour: surely this is what we as civilised people should be doing.

Sources

The Lucifer Effect: How Good People Turn Evil, by Philip Zimbardo (2007)

> *"Trust Allah but tie up your camel."*
> Arab proverb

Failure

If optimism is the expectation of success, what do we do when we fail? Ignore it? Downplay it? Surely failure unmasks the optimist as the fantasist he claims not to be and proves the pessimist right.

There are several ways in which failure is not only compatible with an optimistic outlook but can enhance it. To be alive is to accept that you will fail sometimes. To expect continuous success is to risk sending yourself into continuous freefall.

The following strategy for successful failure applies to the arts, business, politics, science, future-forecasting and any other area of life in which ambition lurks.

1. *Success and failure are subjective and relative.*

   You could say that failure is just information interpreted by our brains. It is we who load it with connotations and emotions, particularly if we compare ourselves to other people or let them judge us. Curiously, you can succeed in the eyes of the world and still feel like a failure because you are too demanding. Lord Reith, founder of the BBC, for instance, set the bar for himself impossibly high and was perpetually dissatisfied as a result, but is remembered with admiration for his achievements.

   It doesn't help that we live in a culture obsessed by 'performance' and 'targets' and in which criticism (in the negative sense) is the norm: if you sail past your targets a year after your deadline, is that success or failure?

2. *Failure is almost always temporary.*

   Substitute obstacle and setback and you can see it in a different light. Of course, you can die while trying to reach the pole…

3. *There is a lot to learn from failure.*

   Ask any toddler about the truth of this. It's wise not to launch yourself down a black ski run unless you know how to fall over without hurting yourself. Few entrepreneurs succeed first time: they pay attention to their mistakes, refine their products and methods, and wade straight back into the water. To learn from your errors is certainly humbling but it doesn't have to be humiliating. As the song advises:

   > Don't lose your confidence if you slip,
   > be grateful for a pleasant trip,
   > pick yourself up, dust yourself off
   > and start all over again.

   Failure forces us to be flexible, to try another way. If you can't think of anything different to do, try thinking (qv).

4. *Success is much more satisfying if it doesn't come easily (honest).*

   The process of life is at least half the fun. Or as Idries Shah puts it a little wistfully in *The Magic Monastery:* "The expected apricot is never as sweet when it reaches the mouth". If you are the kind of person who likes such cod wisdom dressed up in scientific language, you should consult an expert in psychophysics – "the study of the psychological impact of physical events" – which, says Robert Provine, author of *Laughter: A Scientific Investigation* indicates that:

> "More is not always better, and that greener grass, once acquired, quickly starts to yellow… The second million dollars, like the second Ferrari, does not equal the satisfaction provided by the first, and a second Nobel is pretty much out of the question, a dilemma of past laureates. Goals once obtained become the new standard, to which we adapt, before continuing our race up the escalating, slippery slope of acquisitiveness and fame… Philosophers and scientists from antiquity to the present generally agree that life is a marathon, not a sprint, and the formula for happiness and well-being is the journey — not achievement of the goal — and the comfort of friends and family."

Psychiatrists and religious teachers call the ability to wait for rewards 'delayed gratification' and if you are an averagely adjusted neurotic you should have learned how to delay your own gratification by the age of five. In fact (you're not going to like this if you are hell bent on success) …

5. *Suffering and hardship are what make us grow as individuals.*

According to M. Scott Peck in *The Road Less Traveled*, we just have to get on and take the knocks so that we can emerge stronger the other side. In other words, you should embrace failure. It means you are on the right road.

6. *It is possible to peak too soon.*

Many great artists and writers have done their best work in their 20s and been obliged to live their lives in the knowledge that they will never quite deliver on that early promise or recapture their lost glory.

To be lauded as a genius on the basis of one juvenile work can make your continuing underachievement all the more painful. Tennessee Williams sadly wrote about himself:

> "if only I could get the coloured lights going in my brain!...The talent died in me from overexposure, sort of sunstroke under the baleful sun of success...The way down is long and it continues..."

And, of course, if you live your entire life as a celebrity you can never have normal experiences of what life is really like for the rest of us: the best preparation for writing a great novel is, as Cervantes, discovered 60 years of fighting, imprisonment, poverty and obscurity.

Actually, I should qualify my put-down of early success. David Galenson, economics professor at Chicago University, has defined two types of creative people – experimental and conceptual innovators.

> "Experimental innovators work slowly, try things out, use the methods that work and abandon those that don't. Their masterpieces, like those of Cezanne, tend to come late in their lives. Conceptual innovators, like Picasso, formulate new ideas at an early age."

Although he is talking about artists, the principle could apply just as easily to scientists or anyone else. He calls the young achievers 'finders' – they have "one extraordinary idea before preconceived habits of thought" set in and they use it to break boundaries before they settle down to a slow fade. Late achievers are 'seekers' who are "slow-bubbling, uncertain, cautious, experimental; they believe the essence of creativity lies in the process of making the work" rather than the work itself.

7. *Failure can be a reliable way of discovering what we really want to do or what is best for us.*

Through failing we can refine our objectives. Would you rather be rich, famous and inundated with offers of sex right now even though you know you're a sham or be acclaimed as genius posthumously, your reputation assured for the next couple of millennia? The choice doesn't have to be quite so stark. Isabel Allende, then a journalist now a world-famous novelist, was sent by a magazine to interview the poet Pablo Neruda. When her piece was published, Neruda was disappointed. She was poor at handling facts, he said, perhaps she should try fiction.

So, don't waste time. Get out there and fail. "If I had to live my life over again," said Tallulah Bankhead, "I'd make the same mistakes, only sooner."

Films to make you feel good

For a film to lift up the spirit it is not enough for it to be merely feel-good, funny or sentimental; it has to have edge. There has to be a real chance that things will not turn out well for anyone on screen; that success will elude the protagonist; and that a happy ending might not be reached before the final credits roll.

The film has to be rooted in the real world, not fantasy, and the characters have to have the same chaotic mix of dreams, emotions and weaknesses as the rest of us even if they are magnified and pressure-cooked into 90 minutes of running time. No one on or off the screen is perfect and no one is entirely imperfect either: every true hero is a little flawed and every villain carries within him a glimmer of salvation.

But what we want to see is characters who confront their personalised demons, struggle, learn and make a little progress towards happiness and understanding. It's hard for film-makers to fake such things: we know when we've been conned or when we've really been shown something heartening about the human condition. We leave the cinema knowing that if we keep our ideas clear and stick to our moral guns there is a chance that things will turn out well for us too.

The following is a selection of eight cinematographic journeys through darkness into the light.

✧ *Now Voyager,* Irving Rapper (1942). A love story between a middle-aged spinster (Bette Davis) and a married man which ends happily even though the two agree, for selfless reasons, they can never be together.

✧ *It's a Wonderful Life,* Frank Capra (1946) What would the world be like if you hadn't been born? Worse, of course. The classic feel-good film for Christmas makes the serious point that we should stop bounding between feeling as if we are the centre of the universe and feeling insignificant to the point of suicide, and just play our part in the mechanism of life.

✧ *Witness,* directed by Peter Weir (1985). John Book (Harrison Ford), a good man doing his best in a dirty world, is persecuted for his honesty by his friend who has given in to corruption and takes refuge in an Amish community of upright morality and simple living. There's a stirring scene in which the community works together to raise a barn for one of its members. In the final scene, Book, unarmed, confronts his old friend who could easily shoot him and shames him into submission.

✧ *The Fisher King,* Terry Gillian (1991) What gives the edge to this film about an initially unlikeable man (Jeff Bridges) who falls from grace through his own arrogance and is driven to search for redemption is that it celebrates the imperfection of human beings rather than condemning it or glossing over it.

✧ *Groundhog Day,* Harold Ramis (1993) An unpleasant TV anchorman (Bill Murray) has to relive the same day over and over again until he gets it 'right'. He goes through the whole gamut of possibilities – selfishness, self-destruction – before he realises that the best way to make the best day for himself is through helping other people.

✧ *Schindler's List,* Steven Spielberg (1993) based on Thomas Kenneally's book *Schindler's Ark.* Oskar Schindler was a German businessman during World War Two who risked his wealth, his reputation and his life to ensure the survival of the Jews who worked for him. He works for the Nazi system but remains untainted by it. Heroism and altruism are never simple and the film explores the role conscience can play in a difficult situation.

✧ *Dolores Claiborne,* Taylor Hackford (1995) starring Kathy Bates and Jennifer Jason Leigh. More than the did-she-do-it-or-didn't-she-drama it first appears to be. A daughter who has ostensibly become a successful journalist in the big city comes home to help the mother who she despises face a murder trial. Both the main characters are flawed, in pain, and striving to do the right thing and the morality of the situation is never over-simplified.

✧ *Mar Adentro (The Sea Within),* Alejandro Amenábar, (2004) starring Javier Bardem. The true story of quadriplegic Ramón Sampedro who campaigned for 28 years for the right to die at the time and in the manner of his own choosing. Not a cheerful subject but the film is never morbid or depressing. The ending is strangely positive in that Sampedro gets his wish to face the inevitable in the way he wants.

Flow

If time is the problem – not enough today or tomorrow to get anything serious done, and not enough even in seven decades (see 'Immortality') – what you need is to *get into the flow*. You know, that feeling when things are going exactly as they should; you are concentrated and present in both senses of the word; you have lost your self-consciousness; you've never felt more alive; and you are certain you are going to live forever.

The psychologist Mihaly Csikszentmihalyi calls this feeling 'flow', but it's just a new name for an old phenomenon. In sport it is known as 'being in the zone'; in religion it's called ecstasy or rapture and it is very close to the meditation-induced sense of oneness with the universe promised by eastern mysticism.

Csikszentmihalyi defines it as "effortless concentration and enjoyment...in a self-contained universe where everything is black and white" and "being completely involved in an activity for its own sake. The ego falls away. Time flies. Every action, movement, and thought follows inevitably from the previous one, like playing jazz. Your whole being is involved, and you're using your skills to the utmost." He claims that we can deliberately step into flow if we provide ourselves with the right conditions. Sport and physical activities are most naturally conducive to it but it is easy to get into the flow in a fulfilling job. "Free time," he says, "is more difficult to enjoy than work". Ironically, armed robbery and frontline warfare are also very good ways of dipping the mind into the slipstream of flow. Advanced students of the technique are, apparently, able to find flow on a supermaket checkout till or washing dishes.

But why waste any more time reading about it? If you want to feel flow you need to find an activity which offers the following characteristics, or adapt the activity to conforms to the requirements – let me know if you find a way to make the washing-up challenging and rewarding:

- There are clear goals (and probably rules) so that you know what you have to do. Techniques and ritual can be helpful if you need to give an activity structure.

- It is an activity which demands concentration.

- You are in control. You don't depend on anyone else to carry out the activity.

- The activity offers a challenge which matches your ability level and stretches you just beyond it but doesn't seem unachievable. If you don't feel stretched, increase the challenge. Ideally, you will increase your skills so that you can increase your challenges.

- The activity is rewarding: pleasurable or satisfying.

- You get direct and immediate feedback on your actions: you know whether you are succeeding or failing so you can adjust your behaviour

Sources

Flow: The Psychology of Optimal Experience, by Mihaly Csikszentmihalyi (1990)

Folly

"If people never did silly things nothing intelligent would ever get done."
Ludwig Wittgenstein

In 1998, "four ageing hippies" (according to the press), or artists, sailed across the Atlantic for 63 days from Nova Scotia to Ireland on a homemade vessel described as a cross between a garden shed and a scrap yard put together by the Beverley Hillbillies. "The idea is to show people that you can take the stuff you have around you and recycle it and make use of it, whether its art or a place to live or a way to travel," said one of its crewmembers.

Surprisingly, underneath its patchy plywood exterior *The Son of Town Hall* was a sound and seaworthy vessel but that only serves to illustrate the fact that folly is not always as stupid as it seems.

The world would be far worse without people willing to go beyond the bounds of 'reasonable' behaviour just because they feel like it and it's a shame that eccentricity is not always supported and rewarded as much as conformity. But, thankfully, some people will always do extraordinary things out of inner impulse, often at life-long effort and expense. You might have to search a while to find out about them because they rarely seek fame or publicity: that's not why they do what they do. But they are out there, building improbable buildings and doing strangely beautiful things. I have my eyes open.

Food

There are days when I open the fridge and find there is nothing to eat, but I can't remember a day in my life when I've had *nothing* to eat, which of course is not true for everyone in the world – far from it.

We in the west are not aware how lucky we are. For us, the price of basic foodstuffs relative to income has been dropping for a century and not only can most of us afford at least the basic staples but we also take the miracle of cold storage in the kitchen for granted. No longer do we have to put ourselves to backbreaking drudgery just to earn a crust – literally; no longer are we dependent on harvests or fretful in case some well-fed aristocrat's army should decide to wade through our meagre, ripening field of corn or kill the family cow.

Not only that, food is incredibly easy to obtain: there are shops and supermarkets everywhere and they overflow with edible stuff. We can get a fix whenever we want thanks to the invisible supply chain which moves food night and day from the producer to our nearest shelf in rhythm with our digestive systems.

And there's even more to be grateful for: the choice is bewildering and much of it is prepared for us to take away the labour even of cooking. Spices, once the prerogative of rich households, are cheap and plentiful. If you want to make a religion out of eating there is nothing to stop you converting fresh produce into fetish: "Food has contrived to cross a conceptual barrier from barrier to intellectualism," writes Simon Jenkins in *The Guardian*.

But it gets even better: most of the stuff on the shelves is of good quality and all of it is clearly labelled so that we know what we're stuffing into our insides. You can eat healthily or eat badly: it's entirely up to you.

Above all, you, as consumer, have control. You can buy what is easily available or, if you dedicate the time, go looking for organic produce, or food that hasn't clocked up too many air miles. Or you can show your solidarity with the poor and select fair trade produce even if it is more expensive than supermarket loss-leading own brands.

We really should pause before the check out and bow down to the gods who once used to control the harvests. Every day is harvest day for us.

Sources

Fairtrade: www.fairtrade.org.uk
The One-Straw Revolution, by Masanobu Fukuoka (1978)

Freedom

Many of us alive today in the western world have been born into a life of liberty which would have been unimaginable to our ancestors. It is easy to take such good fortune for granted and just as easy for our rights and privileges to be taken away if we don't constantly affirm them and protect them.

Freedom, of course, varies from country to country, from community to community, and it is often limited by the law for good or bad reasons. A typical selection of freedoms that we enjoy in the western world, and that we should esteem accordingly, is listed over the page.

If you think this is a trite list, you don't have to look far geographically or historically to find a country where some or all of these simple things are or were prohibited. The amount of freedom is probably increasing in the world – often thanks to campaigners and journalists who are willing to risk suffering and death in its name – and if there is one cause we should all be able to rally around, this is it.

Freedoms many people in the west enjoy:

- ✓ To live your sexuality.
- ✓ To marry or not, whether to someone of the same or opposite sex.
- ✓ To say what you want and print what you want.
- ✓ To worship who you want.
- ✓ To be different to everyone else.
- ✓ To criticise your elders and betters, and your religious and political leaders.
- ✓ To do what you want for a living.
- ✓ To go where you want, when you want.
- ✓ To have children or not (for women particularly).
- ✓ To live where you want.
- ✓ To associate with whoever you want for whatever reason.
- ✓ To buy what you want.
- ✓ To dress how you want.
- ✓ To eat what you want.

Sources

How to be Free, by Tom Hodgkinson (2006)

Futurology

> "The human race, to which so many of my readers belong, has been playing at children's games from the beginning... And one of the games to which it is most attached is called 'Keep tomorrow dark', and which is also named...'Cheat the Prophet'. The players listen very carefully and respectfully to all that the clever men have to say about what is to happen in the next generation. The players then wait until all the clever men are dead, and bury them nicely. They then go and do something else. For a race of simple tastes, however, it is great fun."

> GK Chesterton, *The Napoleon of Notting Hill*

We'd all like to know what is going to happen in the future – it's the only way we'll know whether the optimists or the pessimists of the day are right – and vast resources are channelled by politics, science and business into the analytic discipline of future studies (or futurology, not to be confused with astrology), which is an oxymoron if ever there was one, because how can you study that which does not yet exist?

The only materials the futurologist has to work with are the present and the past. His job is to peer into their entrails and come up with predictions divided into the 'three P's and a W': *possible*, *probable*, and *preferable* scenarios for the future, and *wildcards* – unlikely or unforeseeable events.

Historian Donald Sassoon describes the challenge:

> "Guessing the future is a harmless game. To play it properly you need to know what is going on – and for this, and that's the tricky bit, you need to ask the right questions."

One question that most futurologists are not keen to ask is: how well have we done in the past? So let's take a moment to look back over the 'history of the future'.

The future began in the 1950s and 1960s when prosperity and stability in Europe and America enabled people to begin to look forward to a brave new world. Scientists back then were respectable people who did not face ethical choices and they talked of us living under the sea and in space by the 21st century. We were fed visions to match the aspirational times: streets enclosed in glass bubbles, flying cars, personal jet-packs and one-pill meals. An agricultural revolution would feed the Earth's hungry with ease and world government would gradually replace the clumsy apparatus of the nation state. Even warfare would be different: eventually battles would be replaced by state-of-the-art deterrence – the threat of all or nothing obliteration by handsome stainless steel ISBMs.

'The 'future' we have chosen ... reflects our insatiable desire for amusement .'

We set off up a road full of technological promises but got distracted on the way. When man landed on the moon in 1969 , no one thought the chief spin-offs of the nascent space industry would be non-stick frying pans, satellite television and GPS systems to enable motorists to avoid traffic jams. While we crowded round black-and-white television sets to watch the first moon walk, computers were still colossal rooms full of spinning disks. Who really believed then that NASA's clunky Apollo-powered mainframes would, within 20 years, shrink to a PC which could sit onto every desktop in the developed world?

> "Nothing in life is quite as important as you think it is while you are thinking about it."

In 1943 , Thomas J. Watson, president of IBM, is supposed to have declared (although without evidence) "I think there is a world market for maybe five computers". According to cyberlegend, Bill Gates thought the internet had no potential when it first began to connect nerds in bedrooms.

In short, we got a future all right but it wasn't the future anyone was expecting or that the experts were predicting. Of course, it is easy in hindsight to knock soothsayers who get it spectacularly wrong and laud those who prove uncannily right, but we have no way of knowing which is which until the results are in – otherwise we'd all be infallible investors.

But it is worth thinking for a moment about how progress happens. We can dream all we like about inventions that will make our lives better and about sensible steps forward for mankind but what forces actually dictate such things? There are some fairly obvious answers to this question and some less obvious ones. Money is a fairly decisive factor: if someone smells a profit, an invention will get to market; if funds are pumped into an area of research, it will probably produce results. Cosmetic surgery offers a much better rate of return on investment than research into cures for cancer and Alzheimer's.

Sometimes stuff happens because someone can be bothered to do the unpaid groundwork which is necessary for the technology to advance. That we can remove the red eyes from our digital holiday snaps with the aid of a 'mouse' is largely thanks to the hours that spotty teenage boys spent in their bedrooms in the 1970s laboriously programming computers that to the rest of us seemed like machines without any useful purpose.

And sometimes a new technology fails to make any headway simply because it is not as good as the old. As Andrew Marr put it in *The Guardian* when he was trying out various models of 'ebook':

> "Simple technology that works is unlikely to go out of fashion. Those futurologists in the 1960s who predicted a world of silver jumpsuits and food-pills forgot that socks, buttons and saucepans were simple technology that worked. The same is true of books."

There are many forks in the road to the future and our choice of which to take depends on a variety of criteria. It could be argued that the 'future' we have chosen to inhabit today reflects our insatiable desire for amusement – the Nintendo as zenith of civilisation. Perhaps the real-world, non-technological problems were just too big to face and we preferred to invest our time and energy in mobile telephony than techniques to feed the world.

"We are all technological determinists now," wrote Bryan Appleyard in the *The Sunday Times*. "We have no choice. If it can be done, if it flatters human vanity, if it makes money, it will assuredly, be done."

We've allowed progress to be a little more trivial, a little less ambitious than it otherwise might have been. We also seem to have missed our own point: back in the 1960s, we assumed that the point of the future was to make us happier. We saw it as promising safety, reassurance, succour in our old age and help with all our problems. It was somewhere we wanted to get to, a destination in itself. We never thought that the future might become a process, a conveyor belt with no 'stop' button in sight.

But once unleashed, the future picks up its own pace and we cannot help being swept along by constant change. In some ways we are living in an eternal version of Alvin Toffler's 'future shock'. "Now that we have progress so rapid that it can be observed from year to year no one calls it progress," says Stewart Brand, author of *The Clock of the Long Now*. "People call it change, and rather than yearn for it, they brace themselves against its force."

If we can learn anything from the history of predicting the future it is not to lose touch with common sense. There will undoubtedly be spectacular changes to come but the future won't take our pains away. Technology is only ever a help, not a solution. In the western world, the internet has bestowed on us great freedom but it is up to us to work out how best to use that freedom. Far more important than gadgetry in the long run are ideas. If the future has achieved anything so far it is not that we can all isolate ourselves behind computer screens and chat to our friends, but that we as a world are starting to share notions that would have seemed absurd in the 1950s: that everyone in the world should be allowed to benefit from human rights, peace, prosperity, democracy, free choice and the right to pursue happiness however he or she pleases.

Sources

The Black Swan: The Impact of the Highly Improbable, by Nassim Nicholas Taleb (2007)

> "We cannot absolutely prove that those are in error who tell us that society has reached a turning point, that we have seen our best days. But so said all who came before us and with just as much apparent reason."
>
> Macaulay 1830

Gadgets

Most gadgets are more trouble than they are worth. You have to find the damn thing when you need it (and it will always turn up in a bottom drawer three months or three years after you were looking for it); it has to still be in working condition; and you have to remember how it works (I'm sure I kept the instruction book safe, but where?) because the more ingenious gadgets get, the more packed with functions, the more they depend on buttons and menus on pallid LED screens, the more difficult you find it to make them do the simplest thing. (Before you even get to the menu stage, naturally, you have to find some new batteries because of course they have run down since you last used it.) And during this whole preparatory phase you have to remain convinced that the task is worthwhile and that using the gadget will entail less time and effort than you would otherwise have to expend. Has anyone *ever* managed to debobble a jumper, one wonders, with a 'Defuzzer'?

No wonder so many pieces of household equipment – particularly slow cookers and electric carving knives – remain in their unopened boxes, in cupboards, in limbo.

There are alluring gadgets we all buy but never use. Sometimes it is satisfying enough just to marvel at the ingenuity of the thing, to revere the chutzpah of its inventor, to dream about its labour-saving potential, without ever putting it to the test, and perhaps that's because of the unwritten rule of gadgets:

> **Performance never lives up to promise**

If I am ever washed up on a desert island, my one luxury will be a shelf full of assorted gadgets, preferably all solar or coconut-milk powered, but if not, accompanied by a lifetime's supply of batteries. In my infinite leisure time, I'll almost certainly taste the pleasures of shredding my personal data and I won't shrink from using a rotating fork (requires two AA batteries) to wind my spaghetti and keep the tomato sauce off my white shirt.

But then, there are a few essential gadgets to swear by rather than swear at, and more ingenious devices are appearing on the market all the time. If we can learn not to be attracted by glittery things, we can fill our houses and our lives with marvellous little machines that not only do useful things but delight us at the same time. Everyone's list of truly must-have gadgets will be different, but my current favourites are:

1. The bread making machine (an improbable robot which can do a complicated, messy three-process job all by itself).

2. The electric toothbrush (which enables me to check my emails, download songs and write a book at the same time as keeping my molars in shape).

3. Anything at all which runs by itself on renewable energy – which will be the growth area of the future.

H☺ppiness

Happiness used to be something personal, a subject you interrogated yourself about late at night or which you discussed with friends, brows furrowed and a book of poetry to hand: *am I happy? are you happy?*

It certainly wasn't an academic discipline as it is now, an obsession in the public domain; a controversial topic in economics (does capitalism increase or decrease the stock of human misery?) and even the object of respectable policy making – the final frontier of the nanny state is to 'deliver happiness through bureaucracy'.

There are good reasons why happiness never used to be discussed much, apart from it being none of anyone else's business. To begin with, the word is so vague. What exactly are we talking about? The abstract idea of being happy is not pin-downable in any meaningful sense.

And then there is the fact that happiness is very much a luxury good. Ask any subsistence farmer about his plans for next year's happiness and you will realise it is a by-product of good living, a marginal choice which has slipped on to the main shopping list.

Assuming you have earned the surplus capital to sit down and think about such things, you might like to begin with the self-assessment test over the page.

When you refer to happiness do you mean:

- ✩ A succession of pleasant days in a long healthy life.

- ✩ Making the best of whatever comes along and appreciating the free things in life.

- ✩ Loving someone and/or being loved.

- ✩ Enjoying the here and now, and appreciating your good luck and knowing how to exploit it/enjoy it without dwelling on could-have-beens and if-onlys?

- ✩ Accepting your limitations and the limitations of everyone you come into contact with. Being free in your mind of jealousies, envies, regrets etc.

- ✩ Feeling you have a place in the world, in a community, or among friends.

- ✩ Moments of euphoria, joy, ecstasy.

- ✩ Well-being, contentment, satisfaction.

- ✩ Fulfillment: spiritual or otherwise.

- ✩ Freedom (qv): living where you want to live, doing what you want to do.

- ✩ Fairy-tale, happily-ever-after happiness.

- ✩ Self-indulgent, material happiness: a credit card and a shopping centre; a couple of hours in your massage bath (with or without company); or an evening with a take-away and a DVD.

… or some selection or combination of all of the above

… or simply all of the above?

There is no right answer, of course, but if you decide to go chasing after happiness it helps to know what you expect it to look like.

A common assumption is that money brings happiness, or at least can buy it if you know how to spend it in the right places, and certainly if you are rock-bottom poor there is a strong correlation between cash and well-being. But research carried out by Princeton University in 2006 seems to disprove the proposition that as we get richer we also grow happier. "Increases in income have been found to have mainly a transitory effect on individuals' reported life satisfaction," it concludes. Although it is very hard to know how important money is, as the report-writers noted:

> "When people consider the impact of any single factor on their well-being – not only income – they are prone to exaggerate its importance; we refer to this tendency as the focusing illusion. Nothing in life is quite as important as you think it is while you are thinking about it. One conclusion from this research is that people do not know how happy or satisfied they are with their life in the way they know their height or telephone number."

That happiness turns out to a nebulous concept hasn't dampened debate about what contributes to the greatest good for the greatest number and what detracts from it.

The psychologist Oliver James is convinced that prosperity and consumption can make us miserable, even unbalance our minds. In his book *Affluenza* (2007) he argues that in developed countries we have placed –

> "too high a value on money, possessions, appearance - physical and social - and fame. People who put too high a value on these things have been found … to be more likely to suffer from mental illnesses of all kinds…If you place a high value on these things you don't meet your basic psychological needs for intimacy and relationships. Instead you are constantly serving confected wants – the wants that advertisers and big business want you to want. You see yourself as a commodity and you see others as commodities and you try to manipulate them in order to increase your value. That interferes with your intimate relationships…you are obsessed with reward and praise. And you end up, as Erich Fromm said, having rather than being."

If we try to struggle in the spider's web spun around us by capitalism, we only make things worse:

> "The more anxious or depressed we are, the more we must consume, and the more we consume, the more disturbed we become. Consumption holds out the false promise that an internal lack can be fixed by external means. We medicate our misery through buying things…"

James' book was much criticised by free-marketeers

because it seemed to be a challenge to the new Anglo-Saxon economic liberalism which maintains that if people are allowed to be free and prosperous they can make their own arrangements to be happy. It also seemed to revamp the left/right debate about how much society and the state should deliberately try to nurture the well-being of their citizens.

In 2007 Cambridge University researchers published the results of a five-year survey of well-being in 15 European states (the members of the EU in 2004) and found the Danes to be the most contented and the Italians the least. The study reported:

> "Those with the highest levels of happiness also reported the highest levels of trust in their governments, the police and justice system as well as those around them."

In countries without such trust, even the wealthy weren't happy.

As a result of all this attention being paid to feelings of satisfaction and contentment, the countries of the world can now be ranked by Gross National Happiness, a term first used by the King of Bhutan. His Majesty Jigme Singye Wangchuck, "drawing on the Buddhist notion that the ultimate purpose of life is inner happiness...Bhutan's king felt the responsibility to define development in terms of happiness of its people, rather than in terms of an abstract economic measurement such as GNP."

The best place to continue your personal quest for happiness is no longer in your head but on the World

Database of Happiness run by Ruut Veenhoven at Rotterdam's Erasmus University. His website is "an ongoing register of scientific research on the subjective enjoyment of life." It includes a 'Directory of Happiness Investigators', a 'Happiness Bibliography', and a list of criteria useful for judging happiness including consumption levels, the cultural climate (tolerance etc), crime rates (and law and order), education, freedom, health, wealth and inequality, lifestyle, quality of institutions (politics etc), and values.

The next great consumer boom, then, will be in selling happiness. With money, you can buy a peerage, a bespoke education for your offspring and the cosmetic operation you have always dreamed of in the hospital of your choice. All that's left is to choose where you are going to live according to the GNH league tables: never mind that you don't speak the language, you're still guaranteed to be happy there.

Sources

World Database of Happiness:
worlddatabaseofhappiness.eur.nl
Gross International Happinesss:
www.grossinternationalhappiness.org/gnh.html

Helen Keller

Helen Keller (1880-1968) was born deaf and blind but in spite of her disabilities became a successful author and activist on behalf of political and social causes. In 1903 she summed up her attitude to life in an essay entitled *Optimism*. This is an edited extract.

Could we choose our environment, and were desire in human undertakings synonymous with endowment, all men would, I suppose, be optimists. Certainly most of us regard happiness as the proper end of all earthly enterprise. The will to be happy animates alike the philosopher, the prince and the chimney-sweep. No matter how dull, or how mean, or how wise a man is, he feels that happiness is his indisputable right…

Most people measure their happiness in terms of physical pleasure and material possession… If happiness is to be so measured, I who cannot hear or see have every reason to sit in a corner with folded hands and weep. If I am happy in spite of my deprivations, if my happiness is so deep that it is a faith, so thoughtful that it becomes a philosophy of life, — if, in short, I am an optimist, my testimony to the creed of optimism is worth hearing. As sinners stand up in meeting and testify to the goodness of God, so one who is called afflicted may rise up in gladness of conviction and testify to the goodness of life.

Once I knew the depth where no hope was, and darkness lay on the face of all things. Then love came and set my soul free. Once I knew only darkness and stillness. Now I know hope and joy. Once I fretted and beat myself against the wall that shut me in…But a little word from the fingers of another fell into my hand that clutched at emptiness, and my heart leaped to the rapture of living. Night fled before the day of thought, and love and joy and hope came up in a passion of obedience to knowledge. Can anyone who escaped such captivity, who has felt the thrill and glory of freedom, be a pessimist?…Darkness cannot shut me in again. I have had a glimpse of the shore, and can now live by the hope of reaching it.

So my optimism is no mild and unreasoning satisfaction. A poet once said I must be happy because I did not see the bare, cold present, but lived in a beautiful dream. I do live in a beautiful dream; but that dream is the actual, the present, — not cold, but warm; not bare, but furnished with a thousand blessings. The very evil which the poet supposed would be a cruel disillusionment is necessary to the fullest knowledge of joy. Only by contact with evil could I have learned to feel by contrast the beauty of truth and love and goodness.

It is a mistake always to contemplate the good and ignore the evil, because by making people neglectful it lets in disaster. There is a dangerous optimism of ignorance and indifference. It is not enough to say that the twentieth century is the best age in the history of mankind, and to take refuge from the evils of the world in skyey dreams of good. …Optimism that does not count the cost is like a house builded on sand. A man must understand evil and be acquainted with sorrow before he can write himself an optimist and expect others to believe that he has reason for the faith that is in him.

I know what evil is. Once or twice I have wrestled with it, and for a time felt its chilling touch on my life; so

I speak with knowledge when I say that evil is of no consequence, except as a sort of mental gymnastic... My optimism, then, does not rest on the absence of evil, but on a glad belief in the preponderance of good and a willing effort always to cooperate with the good, that it may prevail. I try to increase the power God has given me to see the best in everything and every one, and make that Best a part of my life. The world is sown with good; but unless I turn my glad thoughts into practical living and till my own field, I cannot reap a kernel of the good.

Thus my optimism is grounded in two worlds, myself and what is about me. I demand that the world be good, and lo, it obeys. I proclaim the world good, and facts range themselves to prove my proclamation overwhelmingly true. To what good I open the doors of my being, and jealously shut them against what is bad. Such is the force of this beautiful and willful conviction, it carries itself in the face of all opposition. I am never discouraged by absence of good. I never can be argued into hopelessness. Doubt and mistrust are the mere panic of timid imagination, which the steadfast heart will conquer, and the large mind transcend...

Because I love to labor with my head and my hands, I am an optimist in spite of all. I used to think I should be thwarted in my desire to do something useful. But I have found out that through the ways in which I can make myself useful are few, yet the work open to me is endless.

The test of all beliefs is their practical effect in life. If it is true that optimism compels the world forward, and pessimism retards it, then it is dangerous to propagate a pessimistic philosophy. One who believes that the pain in the world outweighs the joy, and expresses that unhappy conviction, only adds to the pain. ..Behold what the optimist does. He converts a hard legal axiom; he looks behind the dull impassive clay and sees a human soul in bondage, and quietly, resolutely sets about its deliverance. His efforts are victorious. He creates intelligence out of idiocy and proves to the law that the deaf-blind man is a responsible being...No pessimist ever discovered the secrets of the stars, or sailed to an uncharted land, or opened a new heaven to the human spirit...

Every optimist moves along with progress and hastens it, while every pessimist would keep the worlds at a standstill. The consequence of pessimism in the life of a nation is the same as in the life of the individual. Pessimism kills the instinct that urges men to struggle against poverty, ignorance and crime, and dries up all the fountains of joy in the world.

Herd mentality

Logic would tell you that you can never trust a mob to do anything but riot and that only one person (or at most two) can fly a plane at the same time. You certainly wouldn't assemble 5,000 novice pilots on the flight deck of a 747 and ask them to make decisions about which controls to pull to take off and land.

Weirdly, though, experiments have shown that human beings possess the same uncanny sense that enables birds to fly in neat formations without hitting each other and fish to swim at incredible speed in shoals that move as if one mind were controlling them. If you crudely connect an audience of people to a video game, or even a flight simulator, their decisions even out and produce a coherent result which strongly points to the existence of what is called 'collective' or 'symbiotic intelligence' or a 'hive' or 'group mind'.

In *Out of Control*, Kevin Kelly describes a demonstration of co-operative flying by Loren Carpenter, one of the graphics wizards behind Pixar Animation Studios. The members of the audience are asked to land a simulated plane by voting on each movement of the pitch and roll controls with either a red or green wand:

> "There is something both delicious and ludicrous about the notion of having the passengers of a plane collectively fly it. The brute democratic sense of it all is very appealing. As a passenger you get to vote for everything; not only where the group is

headed, but when to trim the flaps… Nobody decided whether to turn left or right, or even to turn at all. Nobody was in charge… The conferees did what birds do: they flocked. But they flocked self-consciously. They responded to an *overview of themselves.*"

This suggests that democracy may not be such a daft way of running a country and that we can trust humanity to make decisions in its own best long-term interests. We may seem bent on division and destruction but when we want to we're also capable of acting with telepathic will.

Sources

Out of Control, by Kevin Kelly (1994)

Hope

Hope and optimism go together but they are not quite the same thing. Václav Havel, former president of the Czech Republic, explores the difference between them in his book *Disturbing the Peace* (1990). Hope, he says, is:

> "A state of mind, not a state of the world. Either we have hope within us or we don't; it is a dimension of the soul; it's not essentially dependent on some particular observation of the world or estimate of the situation. Hope is not prognostication. It is an orientation of the spirit, an orientation of the heart; it transcends the world that is immediately experienced, and is anchored somewhere beyond its horizons.

> Hope, in this deep and powerful sense, is not the same as joy that things are going well, or willingness to invest in enterprises that are obviously headed for early success, but, rather, an ability to work for something because it is good, not just because it stands a chance to succeed. The more unpropitious the situation in which we demonstrate hope, the deeper that hope is. Hope is definitely not the same thing as optimism. It is not the conviction that something will turn out well, but the certainty that something makes sense, regardless of how it turns out. In short, I think that the deepest and most important form of hope, the only one that can keep us above water and urge us to good

works, and the only true source of the breathtaking dimension of the human spirit and its efforts, is something we get, as it were, from 'elsewhere' it is also this hope, above all, which gives us the strength to live and to continually try new things, even in conditions that seem as hopeless as ours do, here and now."

Hope in Christian theology is a virtue, a gift of grace from God, and while the word is rarely used in its religious sense, this does at least indicate that it is a much older, more primal force than optimism.

It is also, as Havel suggests, more enduring because it is a inseparable part of us. No one can force it from you on the rack and you can't leave it by accident on the 10.11 into Waterloo.

Hope is essentially an emotion, not a feeling derived from reason, and it cannot be activated or reactivated by will. It's not interested in received wisdom, realism, statistical proof or argument. It is bravery and foolishness combined, which persists in face of contrary evidence; the motivator behind what seems like a futile effort against the odds; an inner conviction that there is only one way to go whatever the obstacles. It also lies behind the impulse of the artistic creator who is convinced that the world will one day recognise his gifts, who keeps on sending

> *"Hope is an ability to work for something because it is good, not just because it stands a chance to succeed."*

out his manuscripts despite the discouraging feedback he gets.

It trusts in human nature and the human spirit and often implies a belief in, if not a benign god, then at least a sense of purpose and progress to the universe. "We need to remind ourselves more and more often that hope is not a temperament but a virtue, and act hopefully even if we don't feel hopeful," the author Philip Pulman told *Prospect* magazine in 2007.

Optimism is not a virtue or an emotion but a mental calculation; a decision of the mind; a conclusion arrived at entirely by sifting though evidence and experience and applying reason. Whereas hope can be thrown out as a personal belief without justification you need communicable reasons for optimism and these are open to challenge and debate.

Optimism could be said to lie on a continuum of feelings between confidence or expectation and hope. Like hope it trusts in human nature but only through observation of human behaviour.

Whereas hope is more non-committal and vague, leaving the outcome to fate, optimism is more practical in its outlook. Compare "I hope you get better" to "I know/I'm sure you'll get better" or "you are getting better". It could be said that there's something desperate and imploring about hope whereas optimism is more centred, balanced, equanimical. In daily life the two words are often used as if they were interchangeable but it adds richness to the language if we can maintain the distinctions between them.

Human nature

Optimism rests, in part, on a favourable assessment of human nature. This doesn't necessarily mean a blind faith in the goodness of human beings and a disregard for their willingness and capacity to do evil. Rather it comes down to a confidence that human beings always have a range of capabilities at their disposal and that they can and often do choose to act in 'good' or constructive rather than 'bad' or destructive ways.

This is not an assumption which is universally accepted. The debate over the nature of human nature has been raging for as long as people have been thinking. At the moment the fashion is to believe that we are primarily animals like any others, the product of our DNA codebooks, with the environment dictating which genes will be switched on and switched off. This determinist view, in which human beings don't have free choice in a meaningful sense and can only act in a few set ways always for explicable reasons, fits in with a long philosophical tradition of regarding man as a brute who needs to be kept in check for his own good.

There are many variants on this theme but an interesting one is the Nobel Prize winning economist Gary Becker's theory "that all actions, whether working, playing, dating, or mating, have economic motivations and consequences, and can be analysed using economic reasoning" which means that "the economic way of looking at behaviour applies more broadly than originally thought, and people make rational choices about crime, marriage, parenthood, education, even drug addiction."

It's a discomfiting but beguiling idea but runs the risk of monocausalitis – the mental conviction that one cause can explain a multitude of different phenomena. And that's usually the way with any theory which seeks to explain human nature and behaviour.

We are animals but not merely animals. Several things set us apart from our closest relatives, the great apes, not least (we assume) the ability to pose questions about our own nature in language. But even animals behave in ways that are inexplicable and which do not fit comfortably into any scientific theory.

The best we can say is that man is an animal capable of surprising himself and defying his observers. Sometimes we are, it's true, good little book keepers who give all sorts of noble excuses for what we are doing but still devote ourselves to our economic interests. Sometimes we act in mechanistic, biological ways and much of our behaviour can be discussed in purely zoological terms. Sometimes we surprise ourselves with deliberate, bureaucratic acts of cold-blooded cruelty to people who have never done us any harm but every day we engage in small acts of unpaid for and unacknowledged kindness that happen without observation and explanation.

Although scientific evidence suggests that we are all capable of carrying out a commandant's orders to give ourselves an easy life, and even to go voluntarily into the thrilling mire of evil, it is probably not true that we are all as well equipped to practice saintly virtues if given the right context. But the fact that one of us is capable of altruism, philanthropy, mercy, forgiveness or pacifism means that all of us have these powers latent or active within us.

Human nature is, it seems, not to be underestimated. It is stretchable, almost infinitely so. It could be argued that what makes us human is our ability to think, to reason and then to act in ways that are not in our own or our tribe's interests purely because we feel it is the best thing to do. Such a course of action is only possible if we are self-aware, which we are, to greater and lesser degrees and this consciousness that we possess is almost certainly our distinguishing mark.

"If you describe things as better than they are, you are considered to be a romantic; if you describe things as worse than they are, you will be called a realist; and if you describe things exactly as they are, you will be thought of as a satirist."

Quentin Crisp,
The Naked Civil Servant

Humanity, *the rest of*

The fact that you are reading this makes you one of the lucky ones. There are many, many people – consciousnesses like yours and mine, behind eyes like ours – who do not have the leisure to sit down to read a book; the money to buy the book in the first place (or the means to borrow it); or the education to learn how to decypher the code of black symbols in which the book is written. They don't even enjoy a respite from the pangs of hunger which is necessary to concentrate on anything except finding the next meal.

We'll never meet these people. They live in countries we've never been to and never will go to and we only have the faintest idea about their lives through reading newspapers and watching television. We've reclassified their countries from 'third world' to 'underdeveloped' to 'developing' but the terms amount to the same: human societies which aren't doing materially as well as ours.

Whatever name it goes by, this 'other' world is hard to think about. For one thing, it seems unreal. How can anyone be starving when the local supermarket now sells fresh saffron-scented pasta? As Bob Geldof puts it, "to die of want in a world of surplus [is] not only intellectually absurd but equally morally repulsive."

And then, the scale of the problem is just so massive. How can you visualise a billion people in a hundred different countries? News correspondents do their best to show us case histories to represent the faceless masses but does that help us understand the problem and its necessary solutions?

Which leaves us feeling vaguely sorry for those less fortunate than ourselves; vaguely guilty for the way we live; and probably a little indignant on behalf of those who suffer towards those we perceive as causing or exacerbating the problem: corrupt elites, repressive regimes, greedy multinationals or whoever.

Primed with compassion, you can do your bit. If you give a little of your time and money, change your consumer habits and buy fair trade produce, you will certainly be able to mildly improve half a dozen lifestyles elsewhere on the globe without causing much of a dent in your own. But if humanity wants to make an impression on the big kahuna of world poverty, it is going to need something more than individual voluntary effort.

So, the optimist must ask several questions: are we, as a human race, doing enough? Are things getting better? Are underdeveloped countries developing? More importantly: are lives being improved?

To answer these questions it is necessary to make several mental adjustments to our perception of the problem:

Mental adjustments

1. Rather than bandy about global statistics we need to have a sense of how these break down into national, local and individual experiences of life and be aware that statistics are never static – there are always rates of change to take into account.

2. To talk about 'the developing world' as a whole is meaningless. The 'developing world' is not one thing but many countries developing at different

rates. More than that, it is many regions, many communities, many families, many individuals all balancing tradition and change as best they can. If we imagine the developing world as one enveloping blanket of seamless misery we do everyone in it a disservice.

3. The word 'developing' may be well-meant but it is slightly loaded in that it implies that all countries should head in a particular direction of progress.

4. It is easy for isolated but all too frequent events like wars and famines to obscure our view of the developing world. What we see on the news does not necessarily reflect the long-term situation.

5. We are connected to 'them'; we share the same world. This is becoming ever more evident with the growth of the internet and it is not just a platitude. Ultimately, our well-being is tied with theirs. The economist Jeffrey Sachs advises us to pay attention to 'the weakest links' if only for our own selfish good.

> "In an interconnected world, all parts of the world are affected by what happens in all other parts of the world, and sometimes surprisingly so. And we are learning to treat them with respect rather than our patronage."

The best example of this interconnectedness is economic migration: if we feel our health, welfare and education systems are overburdened by immigration our best recourse is to create employment in the countries of origin of the migrants. Says Sachs:

> "The way of solving problems requires one fundamental change, a big one, and that is learning that the challenges of our generation are not us versus them... we are living in a cloud of confusion, where we have been told that the greatest challenge on the planet is us versus them, a throwback to a tribalism that we must escape for our own survival."

6.   Charity begins at home. It is a mistake to think that all social problems are far away and that we can help other countries without helping our own poor and disadvantaged.

> "Five countries of Northern Europe have long met the 0.7 percent of GNP commitment."

Jeffrey Sachs points out.

> "These are: Denmark, Luxembourg, the Netherlands, Norway, and Sweden. The striking thing about the aid performance is the very strong correlation between a country's international aid and its care for the poor at home. Countries that take care of their own poor also tend to help the world's poor. Countries that neglect their own poor tend to walk away from their international responsibilities as well. In brief, the social welfare model of Northern Europe helps the poor both at home and abroad."

7.   Our aim should not be to give people in developing countries what we think they need but to empower

them. "You cannot develop people," said Julius Nyerere, first president of Tanzania. "You must allow people to develop themselves."

This is a potentially revolutionary thought as they may not choose to use the power we give them in ways that we like. They may, for instance, reject free market policies and democracy or cling to a religion we consider repressive. But would we want to be told how to run our affairs by some central African country? According to Bob Geldof –

> "The countries that succeed, sometimes admirably, do so by ignoring all the advice of 'the experts' and finding their own culturally appropriate model."

Good development replaces a vicious downward spiral with a virtuous upward spiral, in which all elements work together: healthier people with an increased life expectancy means more workers to build the economy.

8. Money is important but it is not just about money. Sometimes it is about imagination. Says Sachs:

> "One of the odd things about this world I've found in my twenty-five years of work on economic development, is that the war and peace community, so called, and the development community, almost never speak. There are no links between them. If there's a conflict, call in the generals, never call in the hydrologist."

Taking all these provisos into account, it is possible to conclude that things are getting better. According to Indur Goklany, American economist, former delegate to UN intergovernmental panel on climate change, and author of *The Improving State of the World* (Cato Institute, 2007) every objective measure of the human condition is improving even if world population is rising (see 'Poverty' and 'Life expectancy'). And as countries get richer, Goklany claims, they get cleaner, healthier and more environmentally responsible.

It is always necessary and possible for the developed world to do more for the developing world and we must strive for an 'instable equilibrium' whereby we demand more of ourselves but acknowledge what we are doing and what has been done. The future for developing countries is not as good as it could and should be, but is not as bad as it once was.

Sources

The Rough Guide to a Better World, by Martin Wroe and Malcolm Doney, available free from www.dfid.gov.uk

Humour, *a sense of*

It's hardly worth pointing out that it's a sense of humour which keeps us sane and helps us make light of the dark powers in the world. It's also a force not to be underestimated since, in its manifestation as satire and cartoon, it cuts the mighty down to size and questions the puffy sacredness of ideas and institutions, and thus represents the freedom we should all value. Even people living under repressive regimes manage to laugh, sometimes. When we've lost that right, we've lost everything.

> *"An optimist is a fellow who believes a housefly is looking for a way to get out."*
> George Jean Nathan

Immigration

Immigrant workers in western Europe – especially those who have entered the host country illegally – crowd onto the lowest rung of society and at best can expect our indifference, at worst hostility and scorn; but we have much to thank them for and we should admire them rather than insult them. Although some fall to the temptations of crime, or lapse into fanatical religion and even terrorism, the vast majority opt for a peaceful life of hard work, sacrifice and discreet living.

Migrants generally take the anti-social, poorly paid jobs that the host population shun. Most of them want to improve their prospects but they are not on the make. They often spend long periods – years even – away from their families and may not even see their own children grow up. They are vulnerable to exploitation and not usually adequately protected by the health, safety and employment security provisions that we expect.

If they don't "take our jobs" they do take our money – and they spend a chunk of it in a way which benefits the world if we could but see it. The first objective of a migrant worker in a rich economy is to send money back home. "It is my social, moral, cultural duty to help the family," says Sunny Lambe, a Nigerian who lives in London and runs a business to help entrepreneurs. This money he calls "a channel of development" and the World Bank confirms this: the money sent home by migrant workers in the world is equal to around twice the level of official aid that flows into developing countries. An estimated 0.24% of Britain's gross domestic product, for instance, leaves the country not as capital flying from one stock exchange to another, but as cash being invisibly pumped into developing economies.

The irregular free movement of labour in the imperfectly free market of the world, therefore, leads to a free and informal redistribution of at least a small amount of capital towards poor countries. We might want to think about including a few self-effacing, unskilled migrant workers in the next honours list.

Sources

The Hidden Heroes of International Development, by Harriet Harman (2007) available at www.dfid.gov.uk
Immigrants: Your Country Needs Them, by Philippe Legrain (2007)

Immortality

"Baby boomers have always secretly thought that death is optional," remarked Bryan Appleyard, author of *How to Live Forever or Die Trying*, on Radio 4's *Start the Week* in January 2007. His book looks at the 'life-extension movement': an amalgam of scientists who seriously believe that they are on the verge of slowing human ageing or arresting it altogether and thus preventing death. Some such scientists even claim that the children who will live for a thousand years have already been born.

But would you live for a few centuries or forever if you could? Don't answer too quickly. The question has more interesting implications than might at first appear.

Some scientists believe we have a natural maximum life span of 115-120 years but a few maintain that death is not a natural or an inevitable event. Evolution has no interest in us ageing or dying; in fact, it has no interest in what we do after the age of reproduction. Animals – including us – die because something gets us either from without or within. Assuming you can stave off attacks by cars, criminals and wild animals, and death by climatic catastrophe, that leaves the body itself to deal with and there is no reason why every potentially fatal process arising within our organs and our cells shouldn't be checked or even reversed before it finishes us off.

> *"Some scientists believe we have a natural maximum life span of 115-120 years."*

Most people offered the elixir of eternal life say they would only accept it if they could spend the rest of eternity in a youthful body, so science will have to put our body clocks back to 29 years old, but that would be mere elective surgery in comparison to beating death. And if you took the pill, would you want your husband/wife/mother/mother-in-law to take it or would you 'forget' to tell them of its availability so you could avoid an endless lifetime of nagging?

There are a few more catches, too, which might not occur to you until the moment you swallow the medicine and realise there is no going back:

⧗ Boredom (with yourself, above all) and motivation may be problems – why bother to do anything when you have the rest of time to do it in? You can spend the next two hundred years in bed catching up on sleep, but then what?

⧗ Your memory may not cope with the unfamiliar demands made on it: as the cells of your brain are renewed will you still be able to remember who you used to be half a millenia ago? By the time you're 500 or so you'll be able to keep all your family snaps on one nanodisc (not quite large enough to detect with the naked eye and impossible to pick up).

⧗ Of course, you wouldn't be able to have kids because if everyone lives forever and reproduces there will be a population explosion.

⧗ You might have to work beyond retirement age to keep up the payments on your longevity treatment Or perhaps only the wealthy will be left alive, having at last got the only thing that money used not to be able to buy.

⧖ If you are still interested, read the small print before you sign. When some scientists talk about keeping human beings alive indefinitely they assume we won't mind being merged with machines to reduce the number of moving parts and other ephemeral biocomponents which are expensive to replace.

And by the way, you might want to wait a few hundred years to find out which way the universe is developing before making up your mind about being immortal.

But there is a more serious problem with the concept of staying alive past our sell-by dates: it could be argued that to be human is to be mortal. Our perception of the world is based on time, progress and decay. Most of art is predicated on ephemerality and vulnerability. Flowers are beautiful because we know they won't be the same tomorrow. Would we dare to fall in love with another human being, knowing that it means forever?

Alternatively, you could opt for the traditional and much cheaper method of immortality: sexual reproduction – an enjoyable process by which a selection of your cells (hopefully, a 'best of') mingle with those of a loved one to carry part of the physical 'you' into the future.

Sources

How to Live Forever or Die Trying, by Bryan Appleyard (2007)

India

Some countries, you would think, shouldn't work. India is the world's seventh largest country, the second most populous (1,028 million inhabitants – 30 million more men than women) speaking 22 official languages (and 844 dialects), and has the second largest workforce on the planet. It is self-sufficient in agricultural production and yet is still the tenth most industrialised country in the world – one of the six fastest growing economies – with the world's second largest road network and fourth largest rail network. It has its share of absolute poverty and yet is a nuclear power and the sixth nation to have gone into outer space. It has many internal social and religious divisions, and a troubled history of violence arising out of them, but still manages to be the world's largest democracy. The fact that such a country can exist and function should give us all hope.

Sources

National Portal of India: www.india.gov.in

Intelligence

You may not believe this if you watch a lot of television, but the world is getting cleverer not more stupid. There used to be a scientific consensus that educated, intelligent women would choose to have fewer children as they pursued careers, allowing the brainless ones to outbreed them. Thus evolution would come down to the survival of the thickest. But moral philosopher James Flynn has proved this incorrect: IQ levels are rising in the developed world, although he advises us to see intelligence in a less rigid, less mental way:

> "We've got better in those areas that society values. Over the last 100 years, we've come to revere science, and the world has become a place to classify rather than manipulate. For instance, if you'd asked someone in the late 19th century about the link between dogs and rabbits, they'd have answered that dogs were used to catch rabbits. That answer would give you no points in an IQ test, because we're expected to say they are both mammals. This doesn't mean that our forebears didn't know they were both mammals; it's just they would have considered that too trivial a similarity to mention... we are now much more in the habit of thinking in abstract terms. People are now much more open to moral debates, because that's what society takes seriously..."

We are, fortunately, coming to a more rounded concept of intelligence, which begins with some important distinctions. Howard Gardner argues that intelligence is not singular but multiple and he breaks it down into a list of basic forms which do not have to be separate from each other:

1. Logical/Mathematical intelligence – what has traditionally been thought of as intelligence and which, together with the next item forms the basis of western academic education

2. Verbal/Linguistic intelligence

3. Visual or spatial intelligence - the kind an architect or artist might display

4. Musical intelligence

5. Interpersonal intelligence – the ability to relate to others

6. Intrapersonal intelligence – the ability to relate, as it were, to oneself

7. Bodily/kinesthetic intelligence – in which athletes excel

8. Naturalist intelligence – crudely, the ability to read the natural world

9. Existential intelligence – the ability to pose the big questions about the nature of life

Particularly important to another writer on psychology, Daniel Goleman, is that we emphasise the concept of 'emotional intelligence' (similar to Gardner's 'personal' intelligences), which is defined as "being able to have the right degree of emotion at the right time for the right reason for the right duration". Many reasonable people find it difficult to discuss feeling because it is the direct opposite of knowing in the empirical, testable, repeatable, demonstrable sense that science is based on. But if we want to reduce the level of violence and conflict in the world, we'll need to pay much more attention to emotion, and in particular 'anger management'.

All of this takes us a useful step away from the Enlightenment conflation of intelligence with the mental, left-brain ability to dissect reality into its mechanically connected components. It may, with determination, enable us to address the growing divide between scientists and non-scientists. Many scientists openly deride anyone who does not share their world view as superstitious and ignorant. In return, there is a widespread tendency to ridicule science and mistrust it for its dogmatic insistence on being right. There is ever greater need to instate what C.P. Snow called the 'third culture', a cultural marriage in which science, the social sciences and 'the arts' are equal partners.

We are gradually learning to question the opinions of specialists – as Dr David Butler summed it up in 1969: "The function of the expert is not to be more right than other people, but to be wrong for more sophisticated reasons" – and to listen with attention but wise scepticism to anyone who can demonstrate true intelligence as a holistic, integral quality of mind and being.

Partly because of the internet, and partly thanks to television, we are seeing the re-emergence of the once-lost polymath or 'public intellectual', a man or woman with an eclectic, grazing mind who is capable of speaking to us about complexities in the vernacular; and who has a gift for seeing multi-disciplinary connections and for relating abstractions to everyday life. Such people shrug off categories, challenge orthodoxies and risk ridicule or accusations of eccentricity in order to ask fundamental, even apparently stupid questions and to offer unconventional or unpopular answers. They are motivated not by career advances, respectability, peer adulation or Nobel Prizes but by the furtherance of human understanding. They don't fear not knowing or the thought that they may never be able to know. And they don't care whether the explanation they are looking for is on the back of a Corn Flakes packet or in a statistical table in the journal, *Nature*.

We can and should all strive to keep an open and enquiring mind as an intellectual virtue, that is, a listening mind that is interested in what other minds have to say and rules out no idea merely because it has grown out of one particular tradition, be it science, social policy, poetry or religion. We do not have to rush to judgement and we can re-appraise any judgement we do make. Einstein demonstrated this quality of mind but we can also learn the technique from any young child who asks blunt questions without preconceptions or prejudices.

Sources

Frames of Mind: The Theory of Multiple Intelligences, by Howard Gardner (1983)
Emotional Intelligence, by Daniel Goleman

Internet

You can't write a book these days without referring to the omni-invasive internet, and no book about optimism or the future would be complete without giving an award to this slippery multiverse of bytes which is everywhere and nowhere at the same time.

Personally, I think we should praise the internet in all its manifest diversity and pray that control of it stays out of the hands of governments and corporations.

If I have a twinge of scepticism about the internet it is because:

- it has the power to divide people as well as to unite them. It is uncannily good at spreading messages but it can sometimes give the impression of hosting a global debate when in reality only a small number of voices are being heard. It is at once the town crier for the global village and a ghetto where every wacky and perverse interest group can set up headquarters.

- it encourages creativity of a sort, but it also encourages an infinite amount of indiscriminate mediocrity.

- it sometimes thinks it is the world rather than an electronic representation of it. We mustn't forget to open the curtains sometimes and go out to see real things. This might sound obvious but journalism is in danger of becoming reduced to a desk-bound trawl through web pages in search of news instead of a profession of first-hand reporting.

🖰 it fosters a cut-and-paste culture in which anyone can scavenge enormous amounts of knowledge and reassemble it without understanding it. There's no substitute for original thinking.

But overall, who could doubt that we have an amazing tool at our disposal which is developing all the time. Particularly heartening is the growth of the 'open source' philosophy which could easily have withered as dotcom fortunes were being made.

> *"The study of the past and its follies and failures reveals one surprising ground for optimism. In the long run, the idiots are overthrown or at least they die."*
>
> James O'Donnell,
> The Edge survey 2007

Invention

There are still a few odd items waiting to pop into existence that we can't even imagine but which one day will seem as if they had always existed. Not many though. Human beings are good at inventing things but the more big breakthroughs that are made, the less there can be to come. There are only so many wheels and wheelbarrows to dream up. The rest is refinement and improvement.

In *The Shock of the Old: Technology in Global History Since 1900* David Edgerton insists that nothing significant has been invented in the last 20 years other, perhaps, than the GPS system. Interviewed on the BBC Radio 4's *Today* programme he pointed out that he was sitting at a wooden studio desk, sitting on a chair, talking on the radio and that the newsreader had just mentioned the need to invest in railways and the threat posed by nuclear weapons – all examples of the continuing relevance of old technology.

In a list of the ten inventions which have had most impact on the last 1000 years of human history, published in 1999, the *Economist*, confirmed this verdict. The magazine accepted Francis Bacon's three most important inventions

➡   Gunpower

➡   The magnetic compass

➡   Printing

And added seven more:

➠ Calculus

➠ The steam engine

➠ Flight

➠ Photography

➠ Electricity

➠ Computer

➠ The oral contraceptive, the most recent big invention, which has been around since the 1960s.

Edgerton does, however, concede that we can expect advances in nano technology and bio technology in the future.

Artificial intelligence is widely thought by scientists to offer another potentially creative area and when you buy a car in fifty years' time you could well be served by a virtual sales assistant who doesn't need to earn a commission.

Jobs

I'm convinced that – with a few exceptions – 75% to 95% of everything that happens in offices these days is inessential to the health of the business or to the smooth-running of public administration, and that the main function of work is more to keep our hands and minds busy and to give us somewhere to go each day. If you could only follow your boss around all day with a clipboard and a set of electrodes attached to his scalp, you would see for yourself how much of his day is spent not on sourcing raw materials and making sales but on defending his ego in the next board meeting and deciding where he will next go on holiday. It is the thought of being promoted to the same high-level preoccupations which keeps you churning out reports that no one reads and attending seminars intended to "build your core skills and make you a more effective team player".

You may hate it all at times but you have an extraordinary choice nowadays of where and how you will get bored during daylight hours, which is the essence of having a job.

How things have changed. A couple of centuries ago no one had any choice at all. Your job was decided by your family's fortunes and the pecking order. If your family was rich, your elder brother inherited half of Buckinghamshire (and later he'd get two or three parliamentary seats to play with) while you were glad to be given a small curacy in Wales; your younger brother meekly expected dad to buy him a commission in the army even though he really wanted to be an actor and your youngest brother vanished from view, sent to plant wheat or harvest diamonds in South Africa.

If you came from a middle class family you could choose from three tawdry professions, looked down upon by the upper classes: lawyer, doctor or teacher. Or you joined the family firm – even if you hated selling hosiery it gave you a job for life.

You counted yourself lucky that you were not part of the vast mass of people who had to do unspeakably laborious jobs for hardly any money in conditions of utmost grime, launching their offspring early into conditions of near slavery.

Then suddenly came the bizarre idea that you should do what you want and expect to get paid for it. For a time in the 1970s and 1980s, there was even a belief in Britain that you had the right to be unemployed and get paid for it.

Now there is a bewildering choice of careers available. What would someone in 1930s Britain have made of the choice between working in a call centre or joining the cabin crew of a low-cost airline?

Most of us expect to dictate our own careers. If we don't like where we are or what we're doing we happily switch employer or switch profession. We want to work short hours and enjoy long holidays and retire early with decent pensions. We want to work abroad, or from home. We want the world of work to adapt to us not the other way around. And no one questions any of this because we're all doing it.

And it's not long before we take the next logical step. Why work at all? Sell the house, move somewhere cheaper, give tarot readings for a living or make goat's milk yoghurt or do whatever you enjoy. Give yourself the total lifestyle package. There's only one drawback to doing exactly what you want for a living, as novelist Geoff Dyer puts it: "That's the problem with having a lifetime off – you can never take a couple of days off."

Sources

What Should I Do With My Life? by Po Bronson (2003)
The Worst Jobs in History, by Tony Robinson (2004)

Kennedy's peace speech

On 10 June 1963, a year after the end of the Cuban Missile Crisis, President John F. Kennedy gave a speech to American University which is said to have made his opposite number in the Soviet Union, Nikita Khrushchev, cry with gratitude and admiration. It is widely held to have unblocked the tensions of the Cold War (at least for a time) and have led directly to talks which would result in a nuclear test ban treaty.

Much of what he said – the tone and the sentiments – are still inspiring today, especially as they came out of the mouth of the leader of a superpower. Most significantly, Kennedy praised his enemy (for its efforts in the Second World War) and appealed to his countrymen and women to examine their own consciences rather than point accusing fingers across the world. The speech, as Jeffrey Sachs put it in his 2007 Reith Lecture:

"was not only a scintillating exposition on peace, and not only a challenge to his generation to make peace, but was also part of the process itself, a way of problem solving. Kennedy literally used the speech to make peace. Kennedy's chosen process was ingenious. The entire speech is to his fellow Americans, not to the Soviet Union. He didn't tell the Soviets that they were either with us or against us. He didn't lay down preconditions for negotiations. He didn't make a list of things that the Soviets must do. There were no threats of sanctions. In fact, the opposite was true. The entire speech was about US behavior and US attitudes."

On the following pages is an edited extract.

"There are few earthly things more beautiful than a University," wrote John Masefield, in his tribute to the English universities … He admired the splendid beauty of the university, he said, because it was "a place where those who hate ignorance may strive to know, where those who perceive truth may strive to make others see."

I have, therefore, chosen this time and this place to discuss a topic on which ignorance too often abounds and the truth is too rarely perceived – yet it is the most important topic on earth: world peace.

What kind of peace do I mean? What kind of peace do we seek? Not a Pax Americana enforced on the world by American weapons of war. Not the peace of the grave or the security of the slave. I am talking about genuine peace – the kind of peace that makes life on earth worth living – the kind that enables man and nations to grow and to hope and to build a better life for their children – not merely peace for Americans but peace for all men and women – not merely peace in our time but peace for all time.

I speak of peace because of the new face of war. Total war makes no sense in an age when great powers can maintain large and relatively invulnerable nuclear forces and refuse to surrender without resort to those forces. It makes no sense in an age when a single nuclear weapon contains almost ten times the explosive force delivered by all of the allied air forces in the Second World War. It makes no sense in an age when the deadly poisons produced by a nuclear exchange would be carried by the wind and water and soil and seed to the far corners of the globe and to generations unborn.

Today the expenditure of billions of dollars every year on weapons acquired for the purpose of making sure we never need to use them is essential to keeping the peace. But surely the acquisition of such idle stockpiles – which can only destroy and never create – is not the only, much less the most efficient, means of assuring peace.

I speak of peace, therefore, as the necessary rational end of rational men. I realize that the pursuit of peace is not as dramatic as the pursuit of war – and frequently the words of the pursuer fall on deaf ears. But we have no more urgent task.

Some say that it is useless to speak of world peace or world law or world disarmament – and that it will be useless until the leaders of the Soviet Union adopt a more enlightened attitude. I hope they do. I believe we can help them do it. But I also believe that we must re-examine our own attitude – as individuals and as a Nation – for our attitude is as essential as theirs. And … every thoughtful citizen who despairs of war and wishes to bring peace should begin by looking inward – by examining his own attitude toward the possibilities of peace, toward the Soviet Union, toward the course of the Cold War and toward freedom and peace here at home.

First: Let us examine our attitude toward peace itself. Too many of us think it is impossible. Too many of us think it is unreal. But that is dangerous, defeatist belief. It leads to the conclusion that war is inevitable – that mankind is doomed – that we are gripped by forces we cannot control.

We need not accept that view. Our problems are manmade – therefore, they can be solved by man. And man can be as big as he wants. No problem of human destiny is beyond human beings. Man's reason and spirit have often solved the seemingly unsolvable – and we believe they can do it again.

I am not referring to the absolute, infinite concept of universal peace and goodwill of which some fantasies and fanatics dream. I do not deny the values of hopes and dreams but we merely invite discouragement and incredulity by making that our only and immediate goal.

Let us focus instead on a more practical, more attainable peace – based not on a sudden revolution in human nature but on a gradual evolution in human institutions – on a series of concrete actions and effective agreements which are in the interest of all concerned. There is no single, simple key to this peace – no grand or magic formula to be adopted by one or two powers. Genuine peace must be the product of many nations, the sum of many acts. It must be dynamic, not static, changing to meet the challenge of each new generation. For peace is a process – a way of solving problems.

With such a peace, there will still be quarrels and conflicting interests, as there are within families and nations. World peace, like community peace, does not require that each man love his neighbor – it requires only that they live together in mutual tolerance, submitting their disputes to a just and peaceful settlement. And history teaches us that enmities between nations, as between individuals, do not last forever. However fixed our likes and dislikes may seem the tide of time and events will often bring surprising changes in the relations between nations and neighbors.

So let us persevere. Peace need not be impracticable – and war need not be inevitable. By defining our goal more clearly – by making it seem more manageable and less remote – we can help all peoples to see it, to draw hope from it, and to move irresistibly toward it.

Second: Let us re-examine our attitude toward the Soviet Union … No government or social system is so evil that its people must be considered as lacking in virtue. As Americans, we find communism profoundly repugnant as a negation of personal freedom and dignity. But we can still hail the Russian people for their many achievements – in science and space, in economic and industrial growth, in culture and in acts of courage.

Among the many traits the peoples of our two countries have in common, none is stronger than our mutual abhorrence of war. Almost unique, among the major world powers, we have never been at war with each other. And no nation in the history of battle ever suffered more than the Soviet Union suffered in the course of the Second World War. At least 20 million lost their lives. Countless millions of homes and farms were burned or sacked. A third of the nation's territory, including nearly two thirds of its industrial base, was turned into a wasteland…

So, let us not be blind to our differences – but let us also direct attention to our common interests and to means by which those differences can be resolved. And if we cannot end now our differences, at least we can help make the world safe for diversity. For, in the final analysis, our most basic common link is that we all inhabit this planet. We all breathe the same air. We all cherish our children's future. And we are all mortal… And is not peace, in the last analysis, basically a matter of human rights – the right to live out our lives without fear of devastation – the right to breathe air as nature provided it – the right of future generations to a healthy existence?

Postscript

In his 2007 Reith Lecture, Jeffrey Sachs made extensive reference to Kennedy's speech.

> "History records the results. Khrushchev immediately declared to W. Averell Harriman, the U.S. diplomatic envoy, that the speech was 'the best statement made by any president since Roosevelt', and declared his intention to negotiate a treaty. So successful was Kennedy and his team, led by speechwriter Ted Sorensen … that the speech itself was followed in a mere six weeks by a Partial Nuclear Test Ban Treaty with the Soviet Union, initialed on July 25, 1963. That Test Ban Treaty, history shows, was the turning point of the Cold War, the first step down from the threat of imminent mutual destruction that occurred during the Cuban Missile Crisis, a step that put the world on the path of arms control, then détente, Perestroika, and the end of the Cold War itself. Cooperation had begotten cooperation, in the shadow of the near-Armageddon in Cuba."

The speechwriter, Theodore (Ted) Sorensen was sitting in the audience listening to Sachs. A modest man who plays down his role in Kennedy's moment of glory, Sorensen pointed out that while the sentiments in the speech live on, the vital last paragraph has been ignored. It promises:

> "The United States, as the world knows, will never start a war. We do not want a war. We do

not now expect a war. This generation of Americans has already had enough – more than enough – of war and hate and oppression. We shall be prepared if others wish it. We shall be alert to try to stop it. But we shall also do our part to build a world of peace where the weak are safe and the strong are just."

Knowledge

There has never been a time of human history as well informed as ours. But information is not quite the same thing as knowledge and we'd do well to distinguish between the two. Information becomes knowledge only if we verify its accuracy and store it in our brains.

Knowledge could be said to have two vital aspects to it:

1. the facts themselves
2. access to them

Clearly, the first is useless without the second and what sets our age apart is that we have become expert in organising knowledge and making it available to anyone who wants it, regardless of their life experience or qualifications. The internet has transformed the way we deal with and deliver knowledge and its only drawback is its generosity: there is so much information coming at us that it is not always easy to distill knowledge out of the background static.

Particularly revolutionary is open-source philosophy which dispels the aura of copyright and ownership of knowledge in favour of democratic participation and collective intelligence. The classical scholars of the Renaissance, the great encyclopedia writers of the Enlightenment and the university professors of the Victorian age would all be horrified at the cavalier attitude with which we treat knowledge today but which of us would want to go back to a time when knowledge was kept under guard because of the belief that the mob (i.e. us) wouldn't know what to do with it?

Knowledge is of value for its own sake but can also be useful to us as long as we have the capacity to interpret the facts and decide what to do with them. It helps if we are able to read, and then able to decipher different registers of language including the obscure, pompous, academic and high-falutin'.

But while we are wallowing in the bath of information and knowledge, there are a few traps to be avoided:

1. We must be ready to admit to what we don't know and, more tricky, what we may or will never know. There is no shame in ignorance.

2. We mustn't be overawed by authority – particularly, at present, science – which wants to dictate our course reading list. As the author Mark Vernon warns: "we live in an age that requires the imprimatur of empirical research for it to count as knowledge. Science plays a role not unlike that of the church in the medieval period, having to pass information before it is deemed worthy of trust."

3. In defiance of the dominant, lingering ethic of the Enlightenment we mustn't forget that knowledge is not always acquired from outside ourselves. It is not always 'evidence-based' and rational. We can have self-knowledge, for example. We shouldn't, of course, expect to convince our peers with knowledge that cannot be demonstrated and we will always have to tread carefully through areas which never will produce evidence in the scientific sense, such as politics, law, morality and the clash of human emotions.

4. Knowledge goes in fashions; we should be aware of them and not be taken in by them. An interesting and debatable example of this was given by Jonathan Haidt in response to the *Edge* survey into reasons for scientific optimism:

> "Social sciences are dominated by the preconceptions (obsessions) of baby boomers acquired in their formative years of the 60s and 70s (against a background of women's lib, Vietnam etc.) I have found that conservative ideas (about authority, respect, order, loyalty, purity, and sanctity) illuminate vast territories of moral psychology, territories that have hardly been noticed by psychologists who define morality as consisting exclusively of matters of harm, rights, and justice."

5. As any archaeologist or totalitarian dictator will confirm, knowledge can be lost as well as gained. It can be forgotten by a subsequent generation or civilisation that doesn't value it – are we still able to build a Gothic cathedral? It can be sat upon and not shared: libraries can be locked and books can be burned. It can be obscured by disinformation: this is the purpose of propaganda. Even respectable institutions charged with determining what is and isn't knowledge can suppress what does not suit their interests.

6. More worryingly, knowledge can be ignored. The surgeon Atul Gawande, for instance, has criticised his fellow doctors for not washing their hands enough. The spread of infection is well understood

but doctors are too busy and forget to apply the revolutionary knowledge that cleanliness is part of the miracle of modern medicine and its absence leads to superbugs living in hospitals.

If we can steer clear of all these pitfalls, what we end up with is a growing body of knowledge which belongs to all of humanity and, as Daniel Everett concludes after studying 'primitive' peoples, "there is freedom and security in group knowledge". It would be handy if we could keep a simple list of what knowledge works in practice – capital punishment, for example, continues to be used in the civilised world only because of the ignorance of people who should know better.

Let's hope the internet is leading us into the age of universalised knowledge in which everything worth knowing will be available online, for free, and in which education will take less of an interest in learning facts by rote and more of an interest in the tools of intelligence, discernment, electicism and above all an understanding that parts always amount to wholes.

Life expectancy

In the Middle Ages most people in Britain didn't live beyond 30, now we can expect to live, on average, to almost 78. The global average life expectancy in 1900 was only 31 but now it is 69.1 years for women and 64.9 years for men and rising. Some countries have done spectacularly well. In China life expectancy was 41 in the 1950s, now it is 71. India has improved from 39 to 63 in a similar period. It's true that some countries have not increased longevity and a few have even gone backwards, but overall the trend is good. And this matters greatly, as the economist Jeffrey Sachs explains:

> "Life expectancy at birth is more than a mere statistic on life span. It can tell us how well a country is doing in terms of the availability of food, health care (in particular, child mortality), social and political stability and peace (ie the absence of violence and war). In 1960 over 100 countries had a life expectancy of less than 60; now the number of countries stands at 47 and declining."

Many happy returns.

Little free things in life

- New car, new paint, new anything.
- Two weeks in shorts and t-shirt.
- Live music (all of it, but especially if it's free).
- The first morning or evening when you notice the days are getting longer.
- A perfect piece of fruit.
- The house to yourself.
- The smell of someone cooking for you.
- Arriving to find the table laid.
- Finding a large denomination note in the inside pocket of an old overcoat.
- Arriving at the station or the airport in time to step straight on to the train or plane.
- When the chance of having sex within the hour are over 75% and increasing.
- Baby animals that you have no responsibility for.
- Young men or women (according to preference) in their summer clothes.
- Switching on the television and chancing upon the most interesting programme you have ever watched.
- A gadget which proves indispensable and which is impossible to break, no matter how hard you try.
- A moment of convincing synchronicity.
- Opening a book and realising that you are not going to bed until you have finished it.

Long Now

Why limit your optimism to the near future when you've got thousands of years to play with, or 'the Long Now'? The term was coined by Brian Eno when he moved to New York City and discovered that here and now were not used in the same sense as in his native England. In New York, it meant *this room* and *the next five minutes*.

This case of temporal culture shock contributed the name to an organisation founded by Stewart Brand which looks beyond the forseeable future to the next 10,000 years. The Long Now Foundation was created in 01996 (it counts dates in five digits so as to beat the deca-millennium bug which will take effect in about 8,000 years time) as an antidote to a civilisation which values 'faster/cheaper' over 'slower/better' and which "is revving itself into a pathologically short attention span" because of "the acceleration of technology, the short-horizon perspective of market-driven economics, the next-election perspective of democracies" and "the distractions of personal multi-tasking".

The future is, of course, a myth and as a concrete way of anticipating it the Foundation intends to create a permanent mechanism according to an inspiration by the computer scientist Daniel Hillis:

> "When I was a child, people used to talk about what would happen by the year 2000. For the next thirty years they kept talking about what would happen by the year 2000, and now no one mentions a future date at all. The future has been shrinking by one year per year for my entire life. I

think it is time for us to start a long-term project that gets people thinking past the mental barrier of an ever-shortening future. I would like to propose a large (think Stonehenge) mechanical clock, powered by seasonal temperature changes. It ticks once a year, bongs once a century, and the cuckoo comes out every millennium."

Hillis' first prototype is on display in the Science Museum in London and he is working on his second. It runs on a binary digital-mechanical system which is accurate to one day in 20,000 years but just in case it runs astray it corrects itself by 'phase-locking' to the sun at noon. He has plans to install the definitve 10,000-year clock in a limestone cliff on a mountainside in eastern Nevada where, he hopes, it will inspire visitors to think about time in the same way as photographs from space made them think about the Earth and its environment. Long Now also intends to create a library for the next 10 millennia of which all existing libraries will effectively form a part.

The Long Now Foundation summarizes its philosophy for the future as:

- Serve the long view (and the long viewer)
- Foster responsibility
- Reward patience
- Mind mythic depth
- Ally with competition
- Take no sides
- Leverage longevity

Sources

Long Now Foundation: www.longnow.org

Meaning of life

To the strict Neo-Darwinian – and isn't anyone educated these days supposed to be a Neo-Darwinian? – we're here because we're here. Life on earth was conceived by chance and modern human beings evolved from elementary particles of vivacious slime only by the clockwork tenacity of genes pitted against the environment. We may think; we may ask questions about what we're doing here; but we're still animals and we have only two instructions to carry out: stay alive and copulate with the best partners who will have you. The notion of life having a purpose beyond the frenzied copying (and creative corrupting) of code is absurd.

Religions, in contrast, are all about breathing non-biological significance into the flesh we are composed off: we are here for someone's very good purpose and we are expected to please him and be good. If we're well behaved we win immortality or set ourselves up for a better life next time around.

Now that consumerism has replaced church attendance, most people would probably side with the Neo-Darwinian rationale by default, or come up with some lukewarm, middle-of-the-road formula that amounts to the same thing.

And so we reach the postmodern consensus that you can (and perhaps should) do what you want with the only life you'll ever get; pursue happiness on your own terms without harming anyone; find a job that will keep you in the lifestyle to which you wish to become accustomed; have a couple of kids if you want to; and make sure that you are a nice, but not necessarily interesting person to meet. This is, more or less, the conclusion of professor Terry Eagleton's quest in *The Meaning of Life*.

By the same rationale, if things aren't going well you may as well top yourself – it's your life. Certainly, there's no particular reason to get up tomorrow morning unless fun is going to outweigh friction.

This seems to me a rather limp intellectual assessment of the great adventure of life and a wasted opportunity. It's a bit like not knowing what to do with a valuable birthday present you've been given. This stuff about meaning and morality being personal, private and relative doesn't satisfy me. And I can't see how it gives kids a sense of the purposefulness of life which they can use to struggle against adversity.

Besides, I don't know anyone who behaves as if hedonism were enough itself. You can fornicate your way through youth. You can drink and smoke yourself to an early death because that's what you enjoy doing. But isn't such behaviour less of a courageous philosophical choice and more a way of running away from the demands of life? "I don't know why we are here, but I'm pretty sure that it is not in order to enjoy ourselves," said Ludwig Wittgenstein.

Even Neo-Darwinians and other atheists seem to live as if there were some significance to what they do. Some devote decades to energy-sapping labours which involve no hedonistic or evolutionary gain – like writing books for non-commercial reasons. They may justify their attitudes in terms of satisfying their curiosity, "may as well while I'm here" or making a contribution to human knowledge. But surely, anyone who sees life as pointless, who can see through evolution's brainless game, would not bring kids into this crazy, tooth-and-claw world but would follow Philip Larkin's ultra-cynical dictum: "Get out as early as you can, and don't have any kids yourself."

> "The notion of life having a purpose beyond the frenzied copying of code is absurd."

I suspect that all of us inside think the same thing (except when you wake with a start at 3am and realise you are wasting your life and there isn't another one to come): there must be more to this being alive thing than meets the scientific eye. After all, who's doing the thinking and where did he or she come from? Consciousness and the mind are disconcertingly baffling even to the most celebral and empircal of scientists: you just can't look behind your own eyes, can you? Someone once described human beings as points of light imprisoned in space suits and that's pretty much how it feels for me. How about you?

Supposing, just supposing, by way of a game, we've beamed ourselves down to this planet for some purpose that we can't remember, what might it be? We could approach this question with backward logic: if a human life is as it is, what is it trying to tell us?

Life is linear, a journey from egg to apparent extinction. We're not told clearly what, if anything, comes after it – all the depictions of heaven we have are man-written or man-painted – so presumably we're meant to apply ourselves to the task in hand and not waste any time preparing for an afterlife. In other words, it's the process that counts, the journey. This takes billions of forms, depending on our genes, the environment and what you decide to do with your free will. But it has some common ingredients whoever you are, wherever and however you live.

Life could be described as a succession of painful and pleasant experiences, not all of which have anything to do with keeping the organism alive or helping it find a mate in order raise a family. You could see it as an obstacle course through time and space in which you are partially free to choose your own route; you can try and escape hurdles and traps but you won't manage to avoid them all (avoiding one kind of trap you can fall into another) and you will always have to solve your own problems.

According to psychiatrist M. Scott Peck, if life is difficult it is meant to be. Its purpose is for us to grow spiritually; to be able to distinguish between vice and virtue; to identify and pursue our higher interests; it is, in short, a school for the soul. As Zorba the Greek puts it: "Life is trouble. Only death is not. To be alive is to undo your belt and look for trouble."

According to William James what makes life significant is the alchemical marriage of two qualities, which can be summed up as an 'inner' ideal (anything which has meaning for you and compels you to act) and 'outer' strengths of character, such as courage, which enable you to realise that ideal.

If we have incarnated it is in order that we may act and think. We may ask great questions about what we're doing here but we shouldn't fret if the answers take a lifetime to work out. The supra-human universe is, by definition, not describable by the human mind and we must not be satisfied with any incomplete, dogmatic explanation, whether scientific or religious.

Sources

The Meaning of Life, Terry Eagleton (2007)

What Makes a Life Significant, William James (1900)

Science, Religion and the Meaning of Life, Mark Vernon (2006)

The Lazy Man's Guide to Enlightenment, by Thaddeus Golas (1972)

The Book: On the Taboo Against Knowing Who You Are, by Alan Watts (1966)

Heaven: A Traveller's Guide to the Undiscovered Country, by Peter Stanford (2002)

Medicine

The obvious reason for us to be optimistic about medicine is that because it has made so many advances in recent years it can be expected to steam ahead with yet more in the near, middle and distant future. Most, but not all medical scientists expect to be able to mend every human condition eventually: they believe it is only a question of time before the prevention and cure of cancer and dementia become routine. Even ageing and death, they say, will be brought under control by the human brain, the laser and the scalpel.

While I wouldn't want to argue about the achievements of medicine, it has to be pointed out that:

1. Some diseases are still little understood despite consuming enormous research funds; and

2. Growing numbers of people consult 'complementary' practitioners because they are unsatisfied with conventional treatment. No doubt a few such people but not all are deluded; many, if not most, presumably think they are getting something that conventional medicine cannot offer them.

The future is likely to see a much-needed convergence between conventional and complementary medicine, leading to a more holistic understanding of the body, and a clear explanation of the connection between the mind and the body as manifested in psychosomatic illness.

Source

Suburban Shaman: Tales from Medicine's Frontline, by Cecil Helman (2006)

Memory

During the whole of prehistory human beings barely recorded anything about their existence except a few sketchy details in cave shorthand that we can't read; certainly nothing about their daily lives, hopes and fears. Even a hundred years ago, taking notes was laborious – a few static sepia images; evocative entries in a diary written with a quill; corroding items in folk museums are all we have to remember the Edwardians by. Until the 1970s the only means to record the passing days were jerky cine film, reel-to-reel tape or a leaky fountain pen and journal.

But today, you could record every second of your life if you wanted to -- and one man in California is doing just that. As long as there is electricity to keep the batteries recharged you could digitalise your entire reality. You could document your children's complete existence. All this is far, far more efficient than storing memories in your head. And memory-keeping is going to get easier. Devices will get ever smaller and more portable until presumably we'll have webcams implanted in our foreheads to back up our eyes, and lighter-than-air, disposably cheap microphones that we can distribute to our children when they go on holiday so they don't have to regurgitate every detail of what they did or didn't eat.

The only trouble in the future will be that if we keep a real-time memory of each lifetime you will need another entire lifetime to enjoy each of your children's memories.

Men

There must be a temptation for women to ditch men altogether in favour of artificial fertility treatment and a life in which collaboration is rated more highly than infantile competition, but I'm fairly sure they still see something in us. And we're doing our best to prove we're salvageable – we work for female bosses without too many sexist remarks behind their backs; attend births when we would rather be down the pub and can sometimes even be heard talking about our feelings. It would just help if we left the room when decisions are being about war and peace are being taken.

If we're not aware of our faults it's only because evolution never favoured the hunter or warrior who stopped in mid-chase to reflect on the social and moral implications of what he was doing. But beyond our endless rationalising and justifying, we are starting to admit (to ourselves but never to women) that we feel a little lost in a modern world in which violence and wilful destruction have changed from being marks of macho courage to being criminal acts. We'd love to talk to each other in that intimate, mutually-supportive way women do, but come on, don't be pathetic.

> "There must be a temptation for women to ditch men altogether."

We'll get there but we'd get there faster if women would only understand that to make way for them in the world we've had to turn ourselves into schizophrenics: we are expected to be virile, physical, decisive, dominant, raw, animal but to know when to drop the mask, groom ourselves and put on an understanding face. No wonder it's hard for boys at school to see how they can please themselves and everyone else (i.e. the girls and women in their lives) at the same time.

Women are slowly coming around to seeing that boys and men need help to regain their self-confidence in a feminising world – but they don't need help in the same way that women like to be helped and they mustn't suspect they are being patronised. In particular, it is clear that families need fathers and that there would be a lot less juvenile thuggery if there were more male role models around to refer to.

Now that women have had three decades to assert themselves, it's time for them to realise that sensitive men (not the brutes) – men who play with their children and clean the sink – have become the underdogs in sexual politics and the law should positively discriminate in their favour.

Micawber, *Wilkins*

The eponymous hero in Charles Dickens' *David Copperfield* (1849-50) is befriended by a genial but mercurial man, Mr Micawber, modelled on the author's father, who is in debt and always waiting for "something to turn up". Finally he is freed from his debts and becomes a colonial magistrate in Australia. The much-quoted Micawber Principle is:

> *"Annual income twenty pounds, annual expenditure nineteen nineteen six, result happiness. Annual income twenty pounds, annual expenditure twenty pounds ought and six, result misery."*

Millennium Development Goals

In September 2000, 189 world leaders attended the United Nations Millennium Summit, and agreed a set of goals for combating poverty, hunger, disease, illiteracy, environmental degradation and discrimination against women. They set themselves measurable targets and a time limit of 15 years to achieve the eight Millennium Development Goals. The countries of the world are thus committed to work together to:

1. Reduce by half the proportion of people living on less than a dollar a day and reduce by half the proportion of people who suffer from hunger – with the longer-term aim of eradicating extreme poverty completely.

2. Provide a primary education for every boy and girl in the world.

3. Promote gender equality and empower women, beginning with the elimination of gender disparity in education.

4. Reduce by two thirds the mortality rate among children under five years old.

5. Reduce by three quarters the number of women who die in childbirth.

6. Halt and begin to reverse the spread of HIV/AIDS, and the incidence of malaria and other diseases.

7. Take action to protect the environment by incorporating the principles of sustainable development into every country's development

policies; reverse the loss of environmental resources; reduce by half the proportion of people without sustainable access to safe drinking water; and significantly improve lives of at least 100 million slum dwellers, by 2020.

8.   Develop a global partnership for development between countries, which will mean, for example:

- creating an open and fair trading and financial system that is rule-based, predictable and non-discriminatory, paying particular attention to the needs of the least developed countries;

- reducing or cancelling debt;

- increasing aid;

- creating employment for young people;

- making essential drugs affordable to the poorest people (in co-operation with pharmaceutical companies);

- making new technologies – especially IT and communications technologies – available to developing countries (in cooperation with the private sector).

Setting targets, of course, is not the same as meeting them and the UN has a long history of ambitions that were not fulfilled in the timescale envisaged. But it does make progress within the limits of its brief. If it took 11 years to eradicate smallpox instead of the promised 10, surely that is still a success. Any reduction of the suffering in the world at any rate of progress is to be applauded. It is an achievement merely for the international political community to speak as one voice and to set targets at all.

World leaders would not have agreed to these targets had they not thought them feasible. It has been estimated that the cost of meeting them would be equivalent to just 0.3% of world income. The target for reducing poverty, in particular, is likely to be met, although sub-Saharan Africa may lag behind the rest of the world. So far, 43 countries accounting for more than 60% of world population have already met or are on track to meet the goal of cutting hunger in half by 2015. For every statistic there is an achievement to boast of and a challenge to shame us and while the latter should never be ignored, we are not going to help the poor by wallowing in our disgrace. Every small reduction in the figures of world poverty represents drastic, lasting improvements and opportunities to real people.

Sources

UN Millenium Development Goals:
www.un.org/millenniumgoals

Nature

While we're lamenting what we've done to the planet, we sometimes forget that nature is tough and it bounces back. The weeds in my garden are far more successful during a drought than anything I choose to plant. Lay a path and it will start breaking up sooner than you want because of the unstoppable life in the soil. Abandon a mine or factory and it will be consumed by trees and shrubs. I once found an orchid sprouting out of a town centre pavement in Yorkshire.

This doesn't mean that we should give up defending biodiversity; rather we could draw two useful lessons:

1. If we work with nature rather than against it our schemes will be more successful. The easiest plants to cultivate are always those that occur naturally in any area.

2. Nature is always close at hand and there can be as much enjoyment and knowledge to be derived by studying the wildflowers on a wasteland as by visiting an exotic garden.

It's reassuring to realise that nature was around a long time before we were and it will cope with whatever we do to it. As Kevin Kelly says, "The nature of life is to delight in all possible loopholes. It will break any rule it comes up with….the catalog of natural oddities is almost as long as the list of all creatures; every creature is in some way hacking a living by reinterpreting the rules." Which means that if we blow our chances we can expect the next civilisation to be formed by evolved slime moulds or cockroaches.

Nelson Mandela

Anyone who endures any length of time in prison for his or her political beliefs has to be an optimist. In his 1995 autobiography, Mandela wrote:

> "Any man or institution that tries to rob me of my dignity will lose because I will not part with it at any price or under any pressure...I am fundamentally an optimist...Part of being optimistic is keeping one's head pointed toward the sun, one's feet moving forward. There were many dark moments when my faith in humanity was sorely tested, but I would not and could not give myself to despair. That way lay defeat and death."

Networking

Some people recoil from the word 'networking' because they assume it means the practice of attending boring parties solely in order to crawl up to successful people who you hope will be able to give you work at some future date. You can soften the definition by adding that networking in this sense is supposed to be of mutual advantage but this merely implies that everyone is turning everyone else into an exploitable commodity. You're not interested in your interlocutors, only in what you can get out of them.

> "You can enjoy someone's company and still exchange business cards."

But I don't see it that way at all. You could just as easily define networking as "socialising not merely for the sake of chatting or finding out about job opportunities but also for sharing impressions of the world, ideas and information." You can enjoy someone's company and still exchange business cards. And the great thing about the modern world is that it is no longer people in the same industry or town who network: it is possible to make all sorts of inter-disciplinary links with geographical location as the least important determining factor.

The internet, of course, takes networking one significant step further. As millions of individuals make contact with each other in different configurations they form 'webs' that by-pass traditional forms of social control such as religions and governments. This enables news and ideas to flash around the globe, mostly for the good but sometimes for the bad. Networking can be as simple as sending an internet link to a friend or an acquaintance: a thirty second gesture that may contribute to some greater work or even help swing a presidential electoral campaign.

"The world is on the move," says the musician Eno: "communicating and connecting and coalescing into influential blocks which will move power away from national governments with their short time horizons and out into vaguer, more global consensual groups. Something like real democracy (and a fair amount of interim chaos) could be on the horizon."

And we are only at the start of all this. We are seeing the potential for networking grow but we're still in our apprenticeships. Gradually we will refine our skills and learn how to communicate with each other in the most efficient ways.

News, *good*

In 1993, the television news presenter Martyn Lewis suggested that people didn't want to hear all the bad news they were fed daily by newspapers, radio and television. He was derided for his remarks – not all news can be pleasant and palatable, his critics said – but later said he had been misunderstood.

But he had a point. Most of the news *is* bad, for the simple reason that good news is not news. Who wants to read a report saying that every plane landed safely yesterday (again)? Details of a conference painstakingly thrashing out the terms of cohabitation between two obscure communities somewhere in the world would make us yawn. And "nameless stranger does something kind for another nameless stranger" is not the sort of headline that hardboiled editors get enthusiastic about.

The news spreads the impression of a world on the edge of disaster. If we hear of a country in conflict, we assume the whole country is chaotic whereas the truth is almost always that civil war is confined to certain regions. If we're told that there's a drought or famine or serious floods, we find it very hard to localise it, to confine the affected area on the map without extrapolating to the whole of Ethiopia or eastern Africa.

One survey in 2002 found that 80% of the British public believe the 'developing world' to be in a permanent state of disaster. The impression had been formed by well meaning and balanced media reports from the African famines of the 1980s and retained in folk memory. We like to generalise and we find it hard to allow diversity;

to believe that most people across the world live in unspectacular normality most of the time.

Editors and journalists insist that they are only meeting demand by chasing sensation and dredging the dirt out of each story but they could probably still sell newspapers and bring in viewers if they upped the content of cheerful but dull news or spent more time explaining the nuances of complex situations.

Or do readers, listeners and viewers see through it all? "Paradoxically, one of the biggest reasons for being optimistic is that there are systemic flaws in the reported world view," says Chris Anderson, curator of TED Conference. "Certain types of news – for example dramatic disasters and terrorist actions – are massively over-reported. Others – such as scientific progress and meaningful statistical surveys of the state of the world – massively under-reported. Although this leads to major problems such as distortion of rational public policy and a perpetual gnawing fear of apocalypse, it is also reason to be optimistic. Once you realize you're being inadvertently brainwashed to believe things are worse than they are, you can... with a little courage... step out into the sunshine."

But if you prefer the good stuff to the bad stuff you can always read *Positive News* or one of several websites which aim to redress the balance in reporting.

Sources

Positive News: www.positivenews.org.uk.
Great News Network: www.greatnewsnetwork.org

Nukes

The theory was insane: they knew that we knew that they knew we'd only use them if they did first etc. The fact that there was no nuclear war between the USA and the Soviets in the 50s, 60s,70s or 80s, say the Cold War theorists, is proof that MAD (Mutually Assured Destruction) worked. We just had to live with the Damoclesian feeling that the logic could break down at any moment and we'd have four minutes before the last and best firework display we'd ever see.

I was never convinced by the logic of deterrence but the first thing we have to be grateful for is that there have only been two relatively small (!) nuclear bombs used in anger. There have been scary moments – the Cuban Missile Crisis and the bellicose Cruise Missile era in the 1980s – but they passed and most of us don't wake in a cold sweat wondering whether a seagull crossing a radar is going to cause someone to panic and trigger the Third World War.

But now what? The best news would be to hear that all nuclear weapons have been dismantled, never to be assembled again; because even one primed nuclear warhead in existence is too many. But let's be realistic. Here's how the teams in the nuclear division stand:

- There are five states which officially possess nuclear weapons and which have signed up to the nuclear Non-Proliferation Treaty: the United States, Russia, Britain, France and China.

- Israel, India and Pakistan, have developed their own nuclear weapons outside the provisions of the treaty.

- South Africa had a nuclear arsenal for a while but announced it had scrapped it in 1991.

- Three states of the former Soviet Union, the Ukraine, Belarus and Kazakhstan, also had nuclear weapons but have now either sent them back to Russia or scrapped them.

- North Korea, controversially, claims to have nuclear capability and it is alleged that Iran's nuclear power programme is a front for the development of weapons. Several other countries operate nuclear reactors for research or to provide power and could thus go nuclear if they wanted to, but they have chosen not to.

Nuclear weapons have not, therefore, spread as much as they might have since 1945 and there are large areas of the world – including southeast and central Asia, the South Pacific, Latin America and Africa – that have declared themselves nuclear free zones.

There are fewer warheads around today than there once were. The US stockpile peaked in 1966 at 32,193 warheads and is now down to just over 10,000. The Soviet/Russian stockpile reached 40,723 warheads in 1986 and is now down to 8,500. There are balancing factors to add to the statistics such as improved technology (better guidance systems etc.) which mean fewer weapons are needed to do the same job. But, in short, rejoice: we can all still be killed several times over, but not so many times.

The Doomsday Clock, a hypothetical indicator of how close humanity is to destroying itself (midnight representing Armageddon), is currently set at five minutes to midnight, 11.55. The best it has achieved since it was initially set by pessimists in 1947 is 11.43 when the Strategic Arms Reduction Treaty was signed between the USA and the crumbling Soviet Union; but in 1953, when both sides were testing weapons, it reached 11.58.

Sources

Campaign for Nuclear Disarmament: www.cnduk.org
The Bulletin of the Atomic Scientist (BAS) – The Doomsday Clock: www.thebulletin.org

> *"The world does get more humane, and the religion of democracy tends toward permanent increase."*
>
> William James,
> psychologist and philosopher
> (1842-1910)

Old age

When the Beatles sang *When I'm 64* no one ever believed they themselves would ever be 64. John, sadly, died young; George only just missed it; but Paul and Ringo sailed past it and with them all the other survivors of a generation who just won't behave like pensioners are supposed to.

Now, thankfully, attitudes have changed and the onset of old age is getting later. We may snigger when Mick Jagger gyrates suggestively on stage but it doesn't shock us. "You may have to grow older," says a greeting card message, "but you don't have to grow old – or grow up".

And that's tremendous news for those of us following up behind. We don't have to learn to play bowls. We don't have to volunteer for work in an Oxfam shop. We don't have to be boring. Within reason, we can start a new career or adopt a new lifestyle if we want to.

The point was made musically when The Zimmers, a band with a combined age of 3000 and a lead singer 90 years old, entered the top 30 in spring 2007 with their cover version of The Who's *My Generation*. And they weren't the first rocking oldies. The Young at Heart chorus has been doing something similar in Northampton, Massachusetts since 1982 despite its understandably high turnover in personnel.

There is no question that being young is more fun than being old, and that we still need to change the prevailing attitude that the old are a burden on the modern consumer society rather than an asset. In traditional societies, on the other hand, age has always been revered and it will be a sign of the maturing of our own society if we can learn to treat the old not just with begrudging respect but with a sincere recognition that they have got useful things to say to us.

But as the neophiliac babyboomers realize that they are now the elderly, there may be a positive switch of direction. In the summer 2007 a new think tank of senior statesmen, The Elders, was created with the backing of Sir Richard Branson and Peter Gabriel and with Nelson Mandela as its most prominent member. It's good to be reminded that age can bring wisdom, vision, serenity and detachment.

Finally, if you are still dreading growing old, here's a list of a few famous late developers (not including the live and kicking):

- Henri Matisse was still painting after 80.

- Stradivarius was just getting good at 80.

- Frank Lloyd Wright was 91 when the Guggenheim opened in New York (the year of his death).

- Louis Pasteur discovered the vaccine against rabies at 62.

- Bach was at the height of his powers at 65.

- Francis Chichester sailed around the world alone at 65.

- Claude Monet was painting water lilies at 76.

- Tolkien published *The Lord of the Rings* when he was 62.

- Nelson Mandela finished off apartheid aged 72.

- Winston Churchill became war leader at 66.

- Josephine Baker returned to performing at 67.

- Hitchcock was 61 when he made *Psycho*.

- Auguste Piccard descended to 3050m at 69.

- Hokusai is still drawing after 70.

- Compay Segundo found international fame aged 90

Sources

The Elders: www.theelders.org
The Zimmers: www.thezimmersonline.com
Young at Heart Chorus: www.youngatheartchorus.com
Warning (a poem) by Jenny Joseph (1961)

Optimism bias

Optimism isn't always an appropriate or beneficial frame of mind. As the government recognized in its *Green Book, Appraisal and Evaluation in Central Government*, it can be positively harmful when budgeting for a public building project. In official speak "optimism bias is the demonstrated systematic tendency for appraisers to be over-optimistic about key project parameters." Which means that excited civil servants think something is going to cost less than it actually does and "if the project is unique or unusual [the] optimism bias is likely to be high."

The 'optimism bias' applies particularly to

- Capital costs: poor definition of the scope and objectives of a project.

- Works duration: schedules are poorly estimated and risks not allowed for.

- Operating costs.

- Under-delivery of benefits.

Appraisers of projects likely to be infected by the optimism bias are recommended to adjust for this bias as best they can using empirical evidence (i.e. facts rather than hopes) and submit to external review.

Source

The Green Book: greenbook.treasury.gov.uk

Pandora's puzzling present

When mankind stole fire from the Greek gods, Zeus was so angry that he devised the ultimate punishment. Not a plague or brimstone or a nuclear catastrophe but the first woman, Pandora, who was designed as a sex bomb to lie and cheat the pants off any mortal while still keeping them gagging for more.

He offered this femme fatale as a wife to Epimetheus – who had been warned not to accept any presents from Zeus – and sent with her a dowry of a jar or vase ('box' is thought to be a mistranslation by Erasmus). Hermes instructed Pandora never to open this but who could comply with such a prohibition? Wouldn't anything be better than staring at that bloody box on the shelf every day for the rest of your life knowing that you could do anything you want except open it?

Up until this point men had never had to do any work and they were never sick: they lived in perfect peace and harmony. Everything changed when Pandora took the lid off the jar and released all evils into the world. Curiously, only one item wouldn't come out of the jar because it got stuck under the lip, and that was hope.

The obvious lessons of this story are:

- women (not money) are the root of all evil (change Pandora for Eve, and you have the same story). It should be noted, however, that the whole thing was a set-up and if anyone is to blame it should be Zeus not Pandora.

- never accept gifts from gods.

⋎   (of course) never take the lids off jars when you are told not to.

⋎   if you do take the lid off a jar scour it thoroughly before you put the lid back on to make sure nothing important is left inside.

At face value, the Pandora story is a mysogynist apology for the wickedness of mankind but it shouldn't be forgotten that it comes to us via a male author, Hesiod, who might, for all we know, have had personal reasons for mistrusting women. There are, however, many ways to interpret the tale, including a 'damage limitation' theory in which we should rejoice that hope was not released because it is the worst evil of all in that it leads us into false expectations.

The thing is, we do have hope: it isn't still in the jar. One version of the story – as this is reported folk myth and Hesiod's text can't be regarded as a definitive text – is that after she has released all the horrors, Pandora went back and let out hope as an act of compassion and generosity towards mankind. Is not hope at least a little similar to the knowledge which Eve acquired by curiosity in the Garden of Eden, an act by which humanity was condemned to a life of drama and passion instead of an eternity of tedium in paradise?

A more mature way to think about Pandora is metaphorically. The jar could signify the human heart and the lid that kept hope safely sealed in also prevented the rogue nasties from coming back and corrupting it. Pandora, in other words, was wise enough to keep the best gift from Zeus safe at home.

Or could the vase represent the womb, the source of all human beings? Is not the innocent, unborn child hope personified: inexperienced, nurtured by female force, a potential yet to be realized in the world?

Source

Works and Days, Hesiod (700 BC)

'Twixt the optimist and the pessimist
The difference is droll:
The optimist sees the doughnut
But the pessimist sees the hole.

McLandburgh Wilson

Paradigm shift

"The thing I'm most optimistic about," says Steve Grand, artificial life researcher and the creator of Lucy, a robot baby orangutan, "is the strong possibility that we've got everything horribly wrong. All of it. Badly. Once, when I was a young child, I accompanied my father on a car journey around some twisty back lanes in England. Dad wasn't familiar with the area, so I helpfully took the map from him and navigated. Things seemed to be going pretty well for the first half hour, until we found ourselves staring helplessly at a field gate that should have been a major road junction. It turned out that I'd been navigating from entirely the wrong page of the map, and it was sheer coincidence that enough landmarks had matched my expectations for me to believe we were on track."

This is 'paradigm shift', a concept created by Thomas Kuhn to explain the dizzying feeling you get when you have to revise all your assumptions. We're very good at creating theories to explain our world, but history teaches that today's accepted truths are tomorrow's fallacies. There are always phenomena that don't fit the theories of the day. They can be ignored for a while, but eventually some clever sod comes along and suggests we try another, completely different way. We resist, but the new paradigm works better than the old; the fog disperses; and it looks from that point on as if it could never have been any other way.

Sources

The Structure of Scientific Revolutions, Thomas Kuhn (1962)

Particularities

"The Large Hadron Collider at CERN is perhaps the greatest testament to...optimism," Karl Sabbagh, a writer and television producer, said in response to the Edge website's 2007 survey into reasons for scientific optimism.

"Conceived decades ago, absorbing two and a half billion dollars, a collaboration between over 40 countries, designed to accelerate invisible particles to 99.999999% of the speed of light and to create a theoretical entity, the Higgs Boson, for which no evidence exists — if this is not a triumph of optimism over realism, I don't know what is."

After which it would be churlish to say that there is a risk – a remote one, so don't get alarmed – that when the Collider is switched on in May 2008 the whole of creation will be sucked into a manmade black hole. That would be an abrupt end to all optimism but at least we'd be going out with a bang rather than a whimper.

Peacemakers

Any idiot can start an argument and if he – it normally is a *he* – happens to have an army, it's a fairly simple process to declare a war. Deciding not to have a war, on the other hand, scores no political points and doesn't make the crowds cheer. News camera crews do not converge on global calm zones where communities live easily with each other; where ethnic cleansing is a sub-division of the laundry business; and where alms not arms are distributed in back streets and dark alleys.

We say we all hanker after peace, but the truth is that it's a bit of turn-off. Linguistically it's very passive: you can't *declare* peace, *wage* peace or *go to* peace. To be a pacifist is not always a respectable thing. And speaking as a boy, I have to admit that no one I know would want to play peace games with peace toys.

No wonder that history so often paints peace as an almost unnatural breathing space between wars and not the other way around.

I'd like to believe that the two exhausting, all-consuming wars fought between 1914 and 1918, and 1939 and 1945 have convinced us that peace is worth actively pursuing. Endless action replays of war footage give the lie to the old myths of patriotism, heroism and courage. It's true that some people have good wars but civilians – never.

The creation of institutions of international collaboration such as the United Nations and the European Union has given us a framework which seems to be more solid than their forerunner, the League of

Nations. Some people would say that the existence of intercontinental ballistic missiles makes peace possible but I am not convinced by the logic of overkill.

I'd rather give credit to the negotiators who shuttle around the globe in the attempt to resolve conflicts. Some of these people are high-profile statesmen; some of them are only interested in peace because it benefits powerful interests; but others are simply people who see war major or minor as unnecessary. In any case, to be a peace negotiator, particularly in the thickets of the Middle East, you have to be an optimist over the long term.

Conflict resolution is now a respected academic discipline which is generating a huge body of literature; for every flashpoint there is a case study from which the principles of prevention can be drawn. "History is littered with the wars which everybody knew would never happen," said Enoch Powell; the only way to prove this dictum wrong for the future is to expect the worst and address the potential causes as early as we can.

Prosperity, technological advance, globalisation, the end of polarised politics and international electronic connectivity all make war less attractive. And we now understand more about human psychology and behaviour than ever before. We can't stop human beings baring their teeth at each other but we can keep tensions in proportion. In his 2007 Reith Lecture, Jeffrey Sachs addressed this issue:

> "We are not warlike by nature – that is far too simplistic – but we are vulnerable to the allure of war to solve problems… human beings hover between cooperation and conflict. We are actually

primed psychologically, and probably genetically, to co-operate, but only conditionally so. In a situation of low fear, each of us is prone to co-operate and to share – even with a stranger. If they see co-operation on the other side they'll continue to co-operate. Yet if they see defection or cheating on that co-operation they will cheat also.. when…trust evaporates… each of us is primed to revert to conflict, lest we are bettered by the other. If you get into a logic of deep distrust it is very difficult to get out of. Game theorists call this strategy 'Tit for Tat', according to which we co-operate at the outset, but retaliate when co-operation breaks down. The risk, obviously, is an accident, in which co-operation collapses, and both sides get caught in a trap in which conflict becomes a self-fulfilling prophecy. In that all-too-real nightmare, we end up fighting because we fear that the other will fight. This fear is confirmed by fear itself. Wars occur despite the absence of any deeper causes."

There are still wars, and there always will be wars, but they are generally smaller and more contained than they used to be. What is encouraging is the number of modern armies which are only potentially bellicose, spending much of their time in peacekeeping or war prevention.

We are probably not yet ready as a species to unconditionally disarm, but we can dream. In *The Intelligent Universe* (1983) the physicist Sir Fred Hoyle offers an alternative to young men slaughtering other young men on the orders of older men:

"My father was a machine-gunner in the First World War...one of the few who came through the immense Ludendorff attack on 21 March 1918. His machine gun post was overrun, not by the usual few hundred yards but by miles, so that he found himself far within the enemy line. My father told me afterwards that this was his worst moment of the war, because of his ever-present expectation of encountering a lone German, with the prospect that, without the possibility of verbal communication between them, the two would be committed to fight it out to the end in armed combat.

It was some years later that I saw the solution to my father's problem. If you were alone in no-man's land, faced by a German with whom you could not talk intelligibly, the best thing to do ... would be to remove your helmet. If the German then had the wit to do the same you would both perceive the fact that, hidden deliberately by the distinctive helmets, you were both members of the same species, almost as similar as two peas in a pod.

Ever since this early perception I have believed that wars are made possible, not by guns and bombs, not by ships and aircraft, but by uniforms, caps and helmets. Should the day ever come when it is agreed among the nations of the world that all armies shall wear the same uniforms and helmets then I will know for sure that at long last war has been banished from the Earth."

Sir Fred Hoyle, *The Intelligent Universe*

That's at least one piece of legislation for an incoming world government to draft immediately.

Sources

Kings of Peace, Pawns of War, by Harriet Martin (2006).
Swords and Ploughshares: Bringing Peace to the 21st Century, by Paddy Ashdown (2007)
War Prevention Works: 50 Stories of People Resolving Conflict, by Dylan Mathews (2001)

> *"History is littered with the wars which everybody knew would never happen."*
>
> Enoch Powell

Pessimism

"The optimist proclaims that we live in the best of all possible worlds; and the pessimist fears this is true."

James Branch Cabell

For most of human history – until we took control of our own food supply from the gods – it made more sense to be pessimist than an optimist. Anyone who relies on the weather to produce a good harvest is wise to expect the worst and breath a sigh of relief it if happens to be a good year. Is it so stupid, in such circumstances, to believe that the sun might go away out of spite and never come back; that crops might fail because of the dissatisfaction of the rain god; that women and animals might be cursed with infertility because of some petty personality spat in heaven; that children and livestock might die without explanation for who knows what reason or that pestilence or plague might sweep through the land carrying off your kin and leaving your enemies untouched?

> *"Pessimism achieves nothing; builds nothing; it leads only to inertia and resignation."*

You might go through the annual drudgery of sacrifices and rituals as ordained by the witch-doctor but you can never be sure whether the gods are on your side or just mucking about with you out of some warped sense of humour. You only have to look at the soap opera that was Mount Olympus in classical times to see who are the moody, corrupted, grudge-laden, unprincipled, unfeeling ones – certainly not the mortals.

No, until man converted religion into mythology, there wasn't any sense expecting the best. Christianity, in spite of the message of hope offered by its founder, promulgated pessimism as a way of intellectual life until at least the Enlightenment. Believers in the middle ages might have been told that there was a heaven to look forward to but hell was far more vividly imaginable and for good measure. The last judgement and the eternal torment of sinners – the slogan of medieval ecclesiastical law makers was 'life should mean eternal life' – was a favourite theme for tympanum carvings and technicolor stained glass windows.

> *"Optimism is useful in propitious situations. Pessimism is useful in dangerous situations."*

Even as superstition waned and new ideas flourished, there was enough political repression, random and orchestrated violence, and general nastiness around to ensure that pessimism kept a high profile. Every high seemed to be followed – or even accompanied – by an inevitable low. Spain's Golden Age of painting and literature which engendered Velazquez and Cervantes was spurred not by a glorious vision of the future but by a profound sense of depression about it. History, you could say, has been one long bi-polar disorder.

Even the hyperactive, forward-striving, high-achieving, evangelising Victorians were stricken with discouragement. The advance of scientific understanding – particularly Darwinism – meant the end of the belief in a divine plan and of civilisation as a one-way climb out of primitivism. The Bible became a book capable of interpretation, rather than the Book which was not to be questioned. If we were just animals, did we really have the gift of morality or were we just clever at spinning yarns to cover up the tracks of our lustful, sinful genes? Worse, some people speculated, if we could evolve from primeval slime, couldn't we 'devolve' and unravel? The knowledge that the sun was going to burn down to the wick one day, even if in some distant millennium, seemed to confirm the deep Victorian fear that the light in a moral and spiritual sense would similarly fail.

Ironically, the mood of pessimism was motivated by what we now think of as progress. The spread of democracy to involve the uneducated working masses threatened to dilute politics and sanction mob rule. The growth of the railways, the widening availability of electricity, the importation of cheap food – all these improved the lot of ordinary people but demoralised the elite of aristocratic and middle-class writers and thinkers who foresaw the growth of an undiscriminating mass culture. Industrialisation, meanwhile, pumped out pollution and there was even a mild climate change scare at the end of the 19th century but nothing, of course, to compare with our own mother of all climate change scares.

And then came a century with two world wars, two communist revolutions, and two atomic bombs which between them accounted for a literally incalculable loss of life. Shouldn't pessimism, not optimism, be the natural stance of any sane person?

Pessimism certainly chimes with the seen-it-all cynicism of our postmodern times. It is the safe, cool, easy stance to take which fits in well with the mood of materialistic, anti-religionism dominating western intellectual life.

And yet, we don't like to hear too much of it. The outspoken pessimist is accused of having a bad attitude and giving in too easily. Pessimism achieves nothing and builds nothing; it leads only to inertia and resignation. The bad guys are going to win, it says, so get used to it.

A pessimist might retort that optimism is too often forced, manipulated by advertisers or politicians, or religiously inspired and offering false hope – a lie, in effect. That the pessimistic stance might, in certain circumstances, be the

> "History, you could say, has been one long bi-polar disorder."

more accurate one. As Randolph M. Nesse puts it, "Pessimism is not a problem, it is a useful emotional state" which can prevent fool-hardy action. "The tendency to think optimism is superior to pessimism is a deep-rooted illusion. Optimism is useful in propitious situations. Pessimism is useful in dangerous situations."

Which brings us to the era of 'constructive pessimism' as defined by Dr. Norem, author of *The Positive Power of Negative Thinking*. "We need pessimism and optimism in equal measures," said Antonio Gramsci: "one to spur us into action, the other to believe we can succeed."

Foa Dienstag, author of *Pessimism: Philosophy, Ethic, Spirit,* believes that pessimism can be liberating in that it enables us to question the modern orthodoxy that progress can be continual and always proceeds in the right direction. We need to challenge this assumption – in politics, particularly.

It might be, therefore, that we have to learn to mix ourselves cocktails of optimism and pessimism to fit changing circumstances, with enough of the former to encourage us to overcome the obstacles in our way but a proportion of the latter to ensure that we don't underestimate those same obstacles.

Philosophical consolations

Okay, life isn't always that great and you sometimes/often/almost always need cheering up. But one thing you can be sure of is that some great mind has gone through infinitely worse than you and had something to say about it afterwards. In *The Consolations of Philosophy,* Alain de Botton suggests – perhaps only half seriously – how six gurus might respond to six universal sources of angst.

The title is inspired by an earlier work, *The Consolation of Philosophy,* written by St Severinus Boethius while he was on the Ostrogoths' death row. His main conclusion is that we shouldn't look for happiness outside ourselves.

Actually, the closer you look at philosophers, the more you realise how little they have to say about making the best of the human condition. But for what it's worth, overleaf are de Botton's prescribed agony uncles with my summaries of what the great men had to say.

Note: none of these philosophers lived perfect lives so perhaps you shouldn't pay too much attention to what they said.

Source

The Consolations of Philosophy, by Alain de Botton (2000)

If you are	You need to consult	Who'd tell you
unpopular	Socrates	People don't always want to hear the truth; but what are you going to do: tell lies to make them like you?
short of money	Epicurus	Forget selling your soul to earn funds; and forget retail therapy; what you need most of all are some friends
frustrated	Seneca	What other way is there to face life except stoically. You're going to have problems; you're going to die. Get used to it.
inadequate	Montaigne	We're all the same: "I have never seen a greater monster or miracle than myself."
broken hearted	Schopenhauer (one of the most famous pessimists who has lived: he was convinced that we live in the worst of all possible worlds.)	You're better off without him/her/it. Desire is always going to drive you batty. Be reasonable and you won't suffer so much.
ovewhelmed by your problems	Nietzsche (But note that he died mad, so don't pay too much attention to him)	Be a master not a slave.

Plastic

If it isn't animal, vegetable, or mineral it has to belong to what has been called 'the fourth kingdom' of existence, named after its mouldability. Plastic has come a long way since Dr. Leo Baekeland, a Belgian chemist and businessman, gave his name to Bakelite, a solid, shiny black thermoset material that became ubiquitous in the interwar years – the Science Museum in London recently exhibited a Bakelite coffin.

The 30s and 40s became the Poly-Age and during the 50s and 60s plastics of all kinds, now in shiny colours, invaded every area of our lives and were either prized for their sci-fi appearance or condemned with the sneering adjective "plasticky".

But where would we be without plastic? What would you write with? What would your computer look like? Chances are there's plastic in your clock, your shoes, your glasses and throughout your kitchen cupboards.

Tomorrow we'll see even more attractive uses of the stuff, however much we say we'd prefer everything to be made of wood, metal, glass and ceramics. I can't get sentimental about plastics in the way I can about a fine piece of timber but life would be duller, less unbreakable and much more difficult without them.

Sources

Plastics Historical Society:
www.plastiquarian.com/ind3.htm

Politics, *optimistic*

Who's the political optimist? The left- or the right-winger? Traditional political thinking is with Polly Toynbee who recently wrote in *The Guardian:*

> "Optimism is…the progressive tradition. Pessimism is the prerogative of the right, who think human nature is essentially dismal and not amenable to improvement. Optimism is for those who know things can always get better, and it is always governments of the left that drive everything …"

The left looks to future potentiality as a guide to action rather than relying on the evidence of past experience. It advocates idealism rather than pragmatism, and it is not afraid to aim at utopia. Things can always be better, it argues; everything can be improved; and we must experiment with new ways of doing things. Every revolution, it believes, promises to produce a better not worse situation.

A criticism from the right might be that left-wing politicians and governments in practice always turn out to be control-freaks who have so little confidence in human nature that they have to enforce progress and good behaviour through laws. It is the individualist, the entrepreneur, the industrialist, the free-market venturer (a right-winger in conventional terms) who is the optimist according to this argument because he puts his money – not someone else's (the taxpayer's) – where his mouth is and takes a calculated gamble on things coming out right.

Pollyanna

After her father's death, the eponymous protagonist of Eleanor H. Porter's 1913 novel (filmed by Walt Disney in 1960, starring Hayley Mills) is sent to live with her rich aunt in a small New England town. To keep her spirits up, she plays 'The Glad Game', the aim of which is always to look for something to be grateful for in the face of misfortune. Her infallibly cheerful outlook is infectious and everyone in the New England town is transformed by it; but she herself has to face up to the extreme test of losing the use of her legs when she is involved in a car accident.

Many other heroes and heroines of children's literature exhibit a similar positive attitude in order to overcome what seems like the innate pessimism and cynicism of the grown up world. Perhaps it says something about adult attitudes that the word Pollyanna is now used to mean naïve, irrepressible, almost insufferable optimism.

Population

There are six and a half billion human beings on Earth and this figure is expected to rise to 8, 9 or even 10 billion before it peaks. This might be a lot more than the planet was designed to accommodate. It used to be generally agreed – when there were almost 3 billion fewer of us – that the 'population explosion' was the biggest threat facing humanity. The more people, it was reasoned, the less resources there would be to go around and hence the more famine, war, poverty and destitution there would be as human tribes fought it out for space and food. This prediction, however, has not been born out by events; and it's surprising how most of us live in peaceful co-existence despite the noticeable increase in population and, in many places, population density.

Some 'Neo-Malthusians' still say that overbreeding will lead to disaster – isn't climate change merely a delayed reaction on the part of planet Earth, a climactic answer to the question of how many people the planet can support in the lifestyle to which we have grown accustomed?

A counter argument is that numbers alone should give us cause for concern but not for alarm. We have proved highly adaptable as a species and we seem to have proved ourselves capable of beating the logic of the demographic doomsday scenario.

It is highly probable that we can stabilise world population at 7 or 8 billion by non-drastic, voluntary means. We simply have to keep more children alive in developing countries through better nutrition and medicine. There is an inverted logic to this. You would have thought that the more children who survive the bigger the population will grow, but no: if the poor are assured that their children will not die in infancy, they behave as we do and choose to have smaller families. If we address the problem of making poor people richer, healthier, more free and more in control of their lives, the population problem will solve itself.

> *"There are two kinds of optimism, the optimism of people who think they know the future and the optimism of people who believe the future will be more interesting and, if always imperfect, more wonderful than they can imagine...If we are the first kind of optimist we seek to transcend the complexities of life to discover something eternal behind it, something like the imagined view of God. If we are the second, we seek to live and think within the swirl of life; we aim for comprehension and wisdom but have no illusions of transcendence or control."*
>
> Lee Smolin, author of *The Trouble with Physics* Edge survey, 2007

Positive thinking

I once sat through a weekend workshop led by two 'rebirthers' who assured me that the only reason we die is because we believe it is inevitable. Or, to put it another way, if you can keep yourself thinking positively enough, you won't ever have to ring down the curtain and shuffle off the mortal coil. As far as I know, no one has managed to prove this technique in practice: if anyone still believes it, I imagine they will say that any practicant who does die wasn't trying hard enough. There again, I meet people every day who haven't died, so maybe there is something in it.

It is difficult to amass evidence of what the mind can and cannot really achieve but it's certainly a fairly powerful instigator of action which, for most of the time, we use in a reactive rather than proactive way. Positive thinking is the conscious attempt to use the mind to steer reality. Whereas optimism weighs negative or unpleasant thoughts and impressions of the world in the balance, positive thinking deliberately ignores them as they are held to be debilitating or disempowering. This is not necessarily anti-natural. Teachers of positive thinking point out that many of us spend our infancies absorbing negative strictures, and being taught castrating emotions like guilt; to bend our thoughts in the opposite direction is merely restoring a balance.

There are variations of positive thinking that go by many different names including positive psychology, learned optimism, neuro-linguistic programming (NLP) and cognitive behavioural therapy. All of them prescribe slightly different techniques to focus the mind into goal-achieving patterns of thought. The title of one of Wayne Dyer's books is the best summary of the field you could ask for: *You'll See It When You Believe It.*

Positive thinking, in brief, involves setting a goal which must conform to three criteria:

- ☑ You must be clear about what you want to achieve;

- ☑ Your goal has got to be realisable (i.e. potentially within your power), and

- ☑ It mustn't depend on anyone else but you.

It's important that you set an objective test beforehand for knowing when you have achieved your goal. This prevents you getting what you wanted but convincing yourself that it's not really what you wanted.

Finally, you have to take action towards your goal starting from the present moment, not tomorrow. However, there is a school of thought which says that it is enough merely to have a strong, clear intention for it to begin to become real.

A more succinct and nuanced summary of positive thinking might be the maxim: 'When you've made a decision, make it the right one'.

Sources

The Biology of Belief, by Bruce Lipton (2005)
You'll See It When You Believe It, by Wayne Dyer (1995)
Unlimited Power, by Anthony Robbins (1987)
Learned Optimism: How to Change Your Mind and Your Life, by Martin E. P. Seligman (1990)

Poverty as history

The slogan 'Make Poverty History' sounds unrealistic to the point of being naïve, but the fact that it can be pronounced with a straight face is an encouraging sign that human solidarity is growing.

Really poor, abject, extreme poverty is defined as an income of less than one US dollar a day and we should whoop for joy because in May 2007 the World Bank announced that the total number of people in the world who are in this lowest bracket of survival has dropped to under one billion, less than one-sixth of world population. That leaves a lot of desperately destitute people but at least the graph is moving in the right direction.

Prozac

Some people, including Aldous Huxley, think that drug-induced optimism would be the answer to all our woes:

> "If we could sniff or swallow something that would, for five or six hours each day, abolish our solitude as individuals, atone us with our fellows in a glowing exaltation of affection and make life in all its aspects seem not only worth living, but divinely beautiful and significant, and if this heavenly, world-transfiguring drug were of such a kind that we could wake up next morning with a clear head and an undamaged constitution - then, it seems to me, all our problems (and not merely the one small problem of discovering a novel pleasure) would be wholly solved and earth would become paradise."

Introduced in Belgium in 1986 and taken by over 54 million people since then, Prozac was the first in a new class of drug, the selective serotonin reuptake inhibitor (SSRI). It is prescribed for patients with depression in order to increase the availability in the brain of the neurotransmitter serotonin which is believed to regulate our moods.

The manufacturers of Prozac do not claim that it cures depression, only that it alleviates it. Several other drugs also induce temporary optimism, including alcohol. Perhaps the most optimism-inducing of all drugs is Viagra and its imitators.

However, the high from drugs is always temporary, and there can be side effects. More pertinently, mild depression could be considered part of an individual's "biorhythmic" cycle and it can sometimes be nature's way of pointing us towards truths that we must face in other ways. As Emily Dickinson said, "...narcotics cannot still the tooth that nibbles at the soul."

Sources

Prozac: www.prozac.com (take a self-assessment test to see if you are depressed)

Radical hope

What do you do when there is no future? This is the question posed by Jonathan Lear in *Radical Hope: Ethics in the Face of Cultural Devastation*. He looks at the fate of the Crow tribe in North America who were forced to give up their hunting and warring lifestyle at the end of the 19th century. The tribe's chief Plenty Coups summed up the situation in the 1920s:

> "When the buffalo went away the hearts of my people fell to the ground, and they could not lift them up again. After this nothing happened."

When the Crow people were forced to live on a reservation their culture disappeared and every aspect of it became meaningless. There was no equivalent of nomadic hunting and constant war to prove courage and honour. We in our flexible, globalised western world do not understand the finality of being unable to live in a way that brings meaning, hence the chief's words. We inflict cultural death in the greater interest of free trade etc. without really being aware of what it means. Maybe adaptation, flexibility and reinvention are not everything. We can't commit to anything because it will shift beneath us. But not everyone can or wants to change everything all the time.

Tribal people descend into spirals of social problems, deprived of meaning to their lives. They are left with shame, confusion, despair. One Crow woman said "I am trying to live a life I do not understand."

Plenty Coups drew inspiration from a dream which told him that by listening and observing, new ways of living could be possible, in as yet undefined forms. Lear calls this 'radical hope': you don't know what you are going to do or how – perhaps the definition of success is not even clear – but you know you will succeed. More than uncertainty, the hope itself first has to be defined. It doesn't rely on a clearly defined intermediary (God, the government, human ingenuity, providence or the inevitable current of progress, for instance). At the very least this hope avoids falling into despair and raises the possibility that a creative response to cultural death will be found.

> "What makes this hope radical is that it is directed toward a future goodness that transcends the current ability to understand what it is. Radical hope anticipates a good for which those who have the hope as yet lack the appropriate concepts with which to understand it."

It takes courage to express such hope – not traditional courage but a particular kind. We have to act with vigilance but facing uncertainty, without following established paths or being rash, courage in this sense is somewhere between cowardice – turning away from the problem consoling yourself in illusions – and rashness.

One modern application for radical hope could be in the transition from dictatorship to democracy that many countries undergo. Each country has to find its own cultural solution to the challenge of moving from one political system to another. To do that it salvages what it wants or what it can of tradition as a guide through times of discontinuity to create institutions which are inevitably new but which have an echo of familiarity.

Even for those of us living in stable countries, radical hope is a reminder that we shouldn't get complacent. We may not be able to believe that our whole way of life, our way of thinking, our symbols, our meaning could be speedily obliterated but we would do well to defend them just in case.

Forlorn Hope

Most optimists never have to put their beliefs to the test but up until the mid-19th century soldiers engaged in siege warfare could volunteer to join a forlorn hope. As muskets and cannons took 20 to 30 seconds to reload this delay could be put to the advantage of the attacking army. A small group of men, known as a Forlorn Hope, would attack the fortress in order to provoke the defenders into firing their first volley. In theory, this gave the main army several vital seconds to approach and climb the walls before the defenders were ready to fire again. Very few survived the attack of a forlorn hope but to live through one was to be guaranteed promotion. The French term for the forlorn hope is even more evocative: *Les Enfants Perdus* or The Lost Children.

Reading, *bedtime*

If you can't find anything to read, you're not looking hard enough. Even if you discount all (with respect) 'cheap' fiction, all nutty non-fiction books, all specialised and boring treatises on obsessions of little interest to you, that still leaves a lot of books worth reading.

Let's assume you inherit enough money to devote your time to reading every day from 16 years old to 70 (treating any time over that as a bonus): that gives you 2,808 weeks. Probably just enough time to get through a thousand books unless you are a fast reader, and to skim through parts of another thousand. If you are still under 40, you could probably still squeeze in a small library's worth.

But you'd have to be very selective. Even if you confine yourself to reading only books written before your lifetime, you will be turning pages until the moment your eyes dim (but then, thanks to technology, you can continue 'reading' audio books). Think of how many classics there are in English, never mind French, Spanish, German, Chinese, Arabic, Japanese, Russian and all other languages – and you really ought to read books in the original, not in translation, so you will have to set some time aside for language classes.

Cost wouldn't be an obstacle, even if you were on the dole (another way to gain reading time) because the western world is so awash with books some copies have almost lost their value. And there are still libraries to explore, both physical and virtual. Then there is the extraordinary Project Gutenberg which offers 20,000 free books to read on screen or download, and another 80,000 via its affiliates.

To have any chance of getting though even half of the world's classics, you'd have to stop reading the reviews sections of newspapers and magazines – not that you'd have time for them – and you'd have to avoid looking at Amazon or else you'd be aware of the steady stream of good books being produced and your reading list would become, literally, endless.

Don't tell me you have nothing to read. But isn't it a great thought that you will never be short of a good book waiting for your attention. So start early, prioritise, sell the television and don't waste time reading the backs of cereal packets.

Sources to get started

1001 Books You Must Read Before You Die, compiled by more than a hundred literary critics edited by Peter Boxall (2006)

Great Books of the Western World, Mortimer J. Adler (ed): Encyclopedia Britannica. A series comprising all the books you need to read for a rounded, liberal education. The original series, published in 1952, ran to 54 volumes. Now there are 60 volumes making a stack measuring (77.5 x 41.4 x 25.1 cm) containing over 500 works by 150 authors: a total of 37,000 pages.

Reality TV

We're not quite at the point of installing CCTV monitors in our spectacles so that we can watch ourselves living our daily lives, but almost. We'll happily spend hours slouched on the sofa watching other people doing the same banal things as we do. And isn't that what television has been striving for all along: to be a medium for the people about the people?

Thinking people react to reality TV in one of two ways. They either shun it as demeaning to the human spirit or claim that it reveals deep truths about modern society and the human soul. Both points of view are true. We've all seen programmes in which 'ordinary' people are put into embarrassing situations merely for our prurient pleasure. But there are also programmes that are superficially just as voyeuristic but which also make a contribution to human knowledge and understanding.

One of the best uses of the format was to cast Michael Portillo, former hardline Conservative politician, as a single mother on Merseyside in 2003. For a week, he lived the life of Jenny Miner, working as a classroom assistant and a supermarket cashier and balancing the family budget of £80. He emerged humbled and chastened. Even political enemies said that it was a shame he didn't still want to be prime minister now that he had first-hand experience of how real people live.

A similar concept was explored in *The Secret Millionaire* in 2006. In each programme, a rich businessman or woman was sent into a poor neighbourhood undercover to find someone who deserved a gift of money. The premise of the search for the noble poor was cringingly patronizing but invariably, the millionaire's sense of superiority would evaporate when he realized that those who have nothing are far more generous with the little they have (their time, their homes, their few possessions) and far less scheming than those who have more than they need.

Such programmes suggest that not all people working in television are shallow, ratings chasers and that in the future we can look forward to seeing more ingenious, philanthropic applications of the reality TV formula in between the outright dross that is broadcast 24/7.

Religion

Not so long ago, in some countries, you couldn't believe what you wanted, only what you were told. Then the modern enlightened, liberal consensus on freedom of worship was established: in most countries you can do what you want in private, and say what you want in public, as long as you don't hurt anyone else.

Recently, a rather arrogant new atheism has begun to stalk the world with the mission to prove that religion is 'wrong' because the entire world can be explained through rationalism and evolution. Its motivation is understandable, however: we're all frightened by the thought that the young men sitting next to you on the tube might be wired up with explosives because God has sent him on a mission.

But religion is not going to evaporate under the onslaught of reason. "One hundred years from my day there will not be a Bible in the earth except one that is looked upon by an antiquarian curiosity seeker," wrote Voltaire, more than two hundred years ago.

If we are to defuse the situation, we need to keep our heads and not turn against religion. Neither do we need to pander to its every dictate. What's needed is to give religion its proper place and debate its practices without seeking to devalue its principles.

All organised religions have two aspects to them: the inner beliefs of the practicant and the outer forms of practice. The former cannot and should not be questioned or challenged unless they lead to actions in the real world. "'Physical' is not the only criterion of truth," wrote Carl Jung in *Answer to Job*: "there are psychic truths which can be neither explained nor proved nor contested in any physical way. Beliefs of this kind are psychic facts which cannot be contested and need no proof. Religious beliefs are of this type."

The worldly forms of religion, however, can and must be debated by society, lest confusion creeps in. All holy books have been written (and edited) by people even if God has dictated them, and they are therefore open to interpretation. All churches and mosques have been built by men. All priesthoods and ceremonies are likewise human additions to religion. Anyone who claims to speak for fellow believers is misguided because how can anyone speak for the inner beliefs of anyone else? The essence of any religion is always the individual's connection with the numinous: all the rest may aid him in his worship but it is, in the end, superfluous trapping.

It follows from all this that all societies must show respect for all religions but religions must similarly show respect for the societies of which they form a part. Any society or community is essentially political: even if it appears to be a theocracy it will still have a power structure and system of all too human decision making.

We should ensure that the state and the political system, and education, are kept scrupulously free of anyone's religious influence. And we should affirm that religion cannot make the law: to preach violence and murder can never be justified in terms of blasphemy; it is simply an incitement to crime.

In an interview with CNN's Richard Guest in January

2006, the Dalai Lama, leader of the Tibetan Buddhist faith, offered a way forward when he said that what the world needed was not religiosity but "inner secular spirituality". He wouldn't explain this phrase but I suspect that many people – whether religious, agnostic or atheist – who do not or cannot put their personal beliefs into words, understand exactly what he meant.

Sources

The God Delusion, by Richard Dawkins (2006)
God is Not Great, by Christopher Hitchens (2006)
Dalai Lama: www.dalailama.com

Rights

"If an elephant has its foot on the tail of a mouse and you say that you are neutral, the mouse will not appreciate your neutrality."

Archbishop Desmond Tutu

Hollywood isn't known for being a repository of profound thinking but occasionally it can surprise us. In between the photogenic shoulderblades of the film star and goodwill ambassador for the United Nation High Commission for Refugees, Angelina Jolie, there is a tattooed phrase –'know your rights' – which seems at first sight to be a trite and trendy political slogan but which actually hints at a very simple, universal but controversial concept which has been argued over for the last 200 years.

Human beings do not, of course, have rights. That is, they are not born with them, inalienable or otherwise. 'Rights' are a fragile, intangible, rationalist invention of the 18th century. First the American Declaration of Independence (1776) sought to make all men equal and then the French Declaration of the Rights of Man and Citizen (1789) spread the idea in Europe.

The popularity of novels during the 19th century is said to have been one of the prime reasons for rights gaining ground as readers of fiction became vicariously familiar with the no-fault suffering of vulnerable members of society. But there was always someone outspoken and powerful to whom the very idea of a right was a nonsense. Monarchs, aristocratic elites and entrenched economic interests had to be coerced and cajoled into giving up their autocratic powers.

The adoption of the United Nations Universal Declaration of Human Rights in 1948 was certainly a milestone in the history of the common man and woman but a right is still only a right if someone is willing and able to defend it in both word and deed. Rarely has an invention been so widely applied and an international 'law' so widely flaunted.

But even if the Universal Declaration of Human Rights were nothing more than a symbolic gesture – and it is more than that – it would still represent a statement of intent of profound significance to women, children, political prisoners, refugees, homosexuals, disabled people and anyone who is for any reason disempowered. At the very least, it allows us to question dictatorial action and it occasionally forces rights-abusers to account for their actions and change their ways.

Some campaigners would like to extend the concept to animals – domestic, farm and wild – and while this may be a more controversial step, at least discussion of it forces us to question how humane we are or should be to other species.

Sources

Inventing Human Rights: A History, by Lynn Hunt (2007)

Robinson Crusoe assesses his situation

I now began to consider seriously my condition, and the circumstances I was reduced to; and I drew up the state of my affairs in writing, not so much to leave them to any that were to come after me – for I was likely to have but few heirs – as to deliver my thoughts from daily poring over them, and afflicting my mind; and as my reason began now to master my despondency, I began to comfort myself as well as I could, and to set the good against the evil, that I might have something to distinguish my case from worse; and I stated very impartially, like debtor and creditor, the comforts I enjoyed against the miseries I suffered, thus:-

----

Evil: I am cast upon a horrible, desolate island, void of all hope of recovery.

Good: But I am alive; and not drowned, as all my ship's company were.

Evil: I am singled out and separated, as it were, from all the world, to be miserable.

Good: But I am singled out, too, from all the ship's crew, to be spared from death; and He that miraculously saved me from death can deliver me from this condition.

Evil: I am divided from mankind – a solitaire; one banished from human society.

Good: But I am not starved, and perishing on a barren place, affording no sustenance.

Evil: I have no clothes to cover me.

Good: But I am in a hot climate, where, if I had clothes, I could hardly wear them.

Evil: I am without any defence, or means to resist any violence of man or beast.

Good: But I am cast on an island where I see no wild beasts to hurt me, as I saw on the coast of Africa; and what if I had been shipwrecked there?

Evil: I have no soul to speak to or relieve me.

Good: But God wonderfully sent the ship in near enough to the shore, that I have got out as many necessary things as will either supply my wants or enable me to supply myself, even as long as I live.

Upon the whole, here was an undoubted testimony that there was scarce any condition in the world so miserable but there was something negative or something positive to be thankful for in it; and let this stand as a direction from the experience of the most miserable of all conditions in this world: that we may always find in it something to comfort ourselves from, and to set, in the description of good and evil, on the credit side of the account.

Source

Robinson Crusoe, by Daniel Defoe (1719). Excerpt from Chapter IV: 'First Weeks On The Island'

Said/done/written/painted etc. before,
it hasn't all already been

You might get the idea that after modernism there hasn't been much going on in the arts except the endless recycling of everything that has gone before with a huge, clever-clever wink in the eyes of artists as they pocket the cash. But postmodernism isn't the only exhibition in town and the art establishment is not always the best place to look for art.

Some people maintain that there are times of high and low talent and that if we live in the latter we just have to lump it and wait for someone interesting to come along. The truth is that we need to know in which direction to look if we really want to be shaken out of our complacency (which is the point of art).

Or perhaps we need to learn how to look, because art is a metamorphosing substance which doesn't always appear in the guise you last saw it. The computer and the internet have created the conditions for the democratisation of art which enables everyone to share their creations, banal and beautiful, mediocre or meaningful, with the rest of the world.

This same levelling force enables art to bypass the market altogether, for good or bad. The market was always an inconsistent judge of originality, sometimes identifying and financing the Next Big Startling Thing but more often pouring money into *Shrek 3* or *Die Hard 4.0* because of their more reliable payback. For the artist, fame and funding are not always signs of success and a little light starving in a garret is no bad thing.

Scientists

What would you like to hear about scientists? That they soon will have all the answers to the riddles of creation and be able to make you happy by merely stimulating an area of your brain with an electrode? Or that they will one day have to admit they will never understand everything, least of all how to make human beings happy, and that some aspects of existence will always remain a mystery?

Science has good reason to be smug at the moment. It has made a lot of progress in comparatively little time and delivered technology into our homes and into our pockets at an astonishing rate. Scientists are getting to understand the universe and the human body pretty well: aren't half the positive things listed in this book, thanks directly or indirectly to it?

Yet, the odd thing is, that although scientists feel successful they also feel a little disappointed and under-confident. They don't think we give them the credit they deserve. It's not just money in research funds that they want from us but recognition that their way is right. They would like everyone in the world to recognise that science is the only possible source of knowledge. It alone is the rational, evidence-based way of assessing the world and revealing the secret mechanisms of nature.

So why aren't we impressed? A lot of us probably think, like Wittgenstein, that science is becoming the party bore that everyone owes a debt to but doesn't want to socialise with: "Man has to awaken to wonder - and so perhaps do peoples. Science is a way of sending him to sleep again." Scientists would vehemently disagree with this statement – theirs is the way of wonder, they insist and we can't run romantically away from the facts.

That explains the disappointment. The under-confidence comes from a few nagging questions that scientists haven't been able to answer and which they argue about in public like fishwives. Chief of these queries is the biggest of all: where did it all come from? We know everything about the Big Bang that started the universe rolling except what happened in the first, crucial fraction of a second.

The next big poser is how life arose. Neo-Darwinian purists believe that life resulted from a chance chemical reaction and natural selection kicked in. To be brutal, life on earth is just "information technology that has got going by random luck" (Richard Dawkins) or a "chemical scum floating on the surface of a moderate sized planet" (Stephen Hawking).

Several respectable scientists are sceptical about such reductionism. They don't denounce evolution or propose we study mysticism instead of science; they merely point out the improbability of a primeval protein marriage leading to everything we see today. The physicist Sir Fred Hoyle ridiculed what he called the 'junkyard mentality' of scientists and explained his metaphor:

> "A junkyard contains all the bits and pieces of a Boeing 747, dismembered and in disarray. A whirlwind happens to blow through the yard. What is the chance that after its passage a fully assembled 747, ready to fly, will be found

standing there? So small as to be negligible, even if a tornado were to blow through enough junkyards to fill the whole Universe."

Now, no one is suggesting that the Creationists should take over science classes but there is surely a need to keep science in its place. The scientific method is excellent in its appropriate fields, those in which evidence is obtainable and measurable, but it is only one method of interpreting the world. The principle of 'evidence based knowledge' cannot, as some scientists claim, be transferred to every corner of life. There never will be any evidence of you being in love except what you feel. No boffin is going to invent a handy pocket moral calculator which will weigh up the evidence for a tricky ethical stance, And no one in a white coat will ever have reliable enough evidence to tell you which is the right way to vote. For some dilemmas of the human condition you are better off consulting a poet.

What makes me optimistic about scientists is that the realisation is slowly dawning on some of them that there are at least three intertwined ways to make sense of the world: we can take bits of it apart and study them with the rational, evidence-based methodology of science; we can observe working 'wholes' (including the universe), which are more than the sums of their parts; and we can apply our irrational, intuitive, inner faculties where they're likely to yield more useful information than the first two methods.

Modern science has done well so far in its relatively short life. It has succeeded in exposing the flaws in superstition and dogmatic religion and demonstrated the value of testing and observing reality as a way to increase knowledge. Maybe it is on the verge of an explanation for everything, but I doubt it. I think the process of unravelling creation will go on both inside and outside the laboratory and that humility is always a prerequisite for knowing anything.

Sources

The Goldilocks Enigma: Why is the Universe Just Right for Life? by Paul Davies (2006)

The World, the Flesh and the Devil: An Enquiry into the Future of the Three Enemies of the Rational Soul, by John Desmond Bernal (1929)

The Conscious Universe, by Dean Radin (1998) Dean Radin: www.deanradin.com

The Selfish Gene, by Richard Dawkins (1976)

Someone always worse off than you,
there is always

You know your mother/father/husband/wife/warder/companion on an idyllic desert island was right when they told you to *stop complaining* but you've never really paused to think what it means in practice.

There should be an annual publication ranking us all according to our good fortune so we can feel slightly better looking at the names lower down. Couldn't we all be obliged to leave our details on some website and be forced to log on each morning so that a yotta-powered computer can arrange humanity into a dynamic league table – if something awful happens to you during the day you tick the relevant box and slide down a rung; if you've had a good day, you leapfrog the unfortunate who was above you and a nano second later you get a congratulatory email from the Server of Universal Encouragement.

A truly enlightened world government could then tax us progressively and fairly, according to our relative good or bad fortune. Thus, you'd get a tax rebate on the days you feel depressed but when things are really going well you'd have no excuse for giving 99% of your earnings to the poor. The only problem with such a league table of self-satisfaction would be that it would make everybody on the planet feel slightly better except for one poor person…

Songs to put a spring in your step

Some airs to hum to lift your spirits and drive pessimists around you mad.

- *I Will Survive,* by Freddie Perren and Dino Fekaris (1979), performed by Gloria Gaynor. Originally an 'up yours' power mantra for women walking out of a relationship, but the lyrics could work for anyone wanting to assert their independence.

- *Walking on Sunshine,* written by Kimberley Rew (1983), performed by Katrina and the Waves. Fairly banal lyric but the music's perfect for jumping up and down to and playing air guitar.

- *You Can Get It If You Really Want,* by Jimmy Cliff (1972). The first song of the soundtrack of the film 'The Harder They Come' with the message that you can get what you want if you are willing to put in the effort.

- *I Can See Clearly Now,* by Johnny Nash (1972) A pop reggae classic rich in universal metaphor: "it's going to be a bright, bright sunshiny day."

- *Imagine,* by John Lennon (1971). An obligatory, utopian theme tune for the optimist with words that can be adapted, out of context, to any application: Liverpool airport has 'above us only sky' as its slogan. Lennon described it as "anti-religious, anti-nationalistic, anti-conventional, anti-capitalistic song" and "virtually the Communist Manifesto".

- *Don't Worry, Be Happy,* by Bobby McFerrin (1988). The first a capella song to reach No. 1 in the USA, its refrain being a quote from the Indian guru Meher Baba (1894-1969) whose teachings were influential in the west.

- *Always Look On the Bright Side of Life,* by Eric Idle, performed by Monty Python. The musical finale of the film, 'The Life of Brian' (1979), is meant ironically since it is sung by a man being crucified but the song is now frequently used as if it were a life-affirming anthem of optimism. Don't look too closely at the words if you want to cheer yourself up.

- *On the Sunny Side of the Street,* by Jimmy McHugh (1930) performed by Dorothy Fields:

  'Grab your coat, and get your hat,
  Leave your worry on the doorstep,
  Just direct your feet
  To the sunny side of the street.'

- *The Roses of Success,* by Robert and Richard Sherman (1968), from 'Chitty Chitty Bang Bang'. Failure is the best thing that can happen to you:

  'For every big mistake you make be grateful:
  That mistake you'll never make again.
  Every shiny dream that fades and dies
  Generates the steam for two more tries'

  The Sherman brothers also composed another perhaps too cheery 'life philosophy' song, *A Spoonful of Sugar* for the film of 'Mary Poppins'.

Taboos, *the passing of*

Only two species of animal go through the menopause and until recently neither of them used to talk about it. Well, we can't be for sure that the pilot whale doesn't discuss it but women in the 1950s described each other as being "all nerves" instead of suffering from a definable life stage-cum-medical condition.

It's hard to believe that not long ago many of the things we talk about now (particularly to do with sex) were 'untalkaboutable'. It's as if we didn't have the words; but what we really lacked was the honesty, empathy and freedom from shame to ask and answer the really vital questions about human thoughts, feelings and actions. Homosexuality, for example, may as well not have existed – if you were gay you were by definition in the closet.

Talking in itself does not create freedom from persecution but it helps. If we can name names without euphemism, we can put things in their places and defuse tensions. A personal problem aired can become a personal problem that can no longer do us psychological damage. Of course, some taboos exist for a reason but most have evolved merely because we're screwed up and we don't see why the next generation shouldn't be screwed up as well. Fortunately, the Sixties, feminism, psychotherapy, the decline of organized religion and the internet, have led to we in the west revering honesty and openness more than concealment.

Terrorism

What possesses a young man to load a rucksack with DIY explosive, sit down next to a perfect stranger on a tube train and detonate himself without further thought? Does he really believe he's taking a short-cut to paradise?

The everyday, plain-clothed application of calculated violence unnerves us because it is unpredictable, seemingly random. And that's the desired effect; it aims to terrorise ordinary people out of complacency into panic. It wants us to walk in fear and for the authorities to feel impotent.

And our usual reaction is twofold. First, we expect security measures to be heightened, for which we're willing to give up increasing amounts of freedom. Second, we give the military and police ever greater counter-terrorist powers in the belief that they will prevent further attacks. Both of these are necessary responses. Experience, however, shows that terrorism is nothing if not tenacious: it eludes arrests and gets through checkpoints. There has to be a more intelligent, long-term strategy as well.

We can take some comfort from the fact that no terrorist movement endures for ever, even if it always lasts for too long. And we should be aware that no movement has quite the impact the media portrays it as having. Every terrorist act (except in a war zone such as Iraq, where the word terrorism is probably misused) is, by definition, relatively rare and limited in scale and statistically we should worry more about the quotidien dangers of life like crossing the road in front of a drunk driver than about the possibility that the man across the carriage is about to take us to the next life with him.

Instead of living in constant fear, we should devote our energies to understanding what is going on. We're given the impression by politicians, other community leaders and the media (which thrives on hysteria) that terrorism comes out of nowhere; that it is unreasonable – even insane; and that it is evil. This is a misleading oversimplification which does not encourage a peaceful settlement of the problem.

Governments know a great deal about how terrorists think and work but this knowledge is not widely disseminated because to do so would be to lend legitimacy to their motivations. The truth, whatever anyone says in public, is that we always end up talking to terrorists if we can. That doesn't mean giving respectability to their actions or giving in to their demands, but it does mean making an effort to understand what they want. And this is the only way to defuse terrorism.

Terrorism is a more or less calculated act of frustration by those who feel themselves to be disenfranchised – victims – or who believe they are acting on behalf of the victims. All terrorists draw support from quiescent communities of respectable people.

They always justify their actions and believe their own justifications. It is pointless to try to devalue their justification. Rather we should acknowledge its validity, even if we don't approve of it. There are still former IRA terrorists who remain unrepentant about bombing the

British mainland. They were soldiers fighting a war, they say. They believed they were using the only language their enemies would understand.

We may unintentionally contribute to the causes of terrorism. That does not mean we *cause* it, but the long-term goal must be to address the conditions that give rise to it: build bridges, restore trust, give hope. We need to man the security barriers in the meantime, but we mustn't neglect this slow work which may take a generation to pay off.

Sources

The Power of Nightmares, a documentary by Adam Curtis
www.archive.org/details/ThePowerOfNightmares

Therapy

For a number of years, off and on, I have been involved in a sphere of activity which doesn't have a proper name of its own but which I call 'personal development': a loose miscellany of books and workshops which offer readers/participants techniques to make them feel better about themselves.

What I have learned from a lot of people spending weekends together in stuffy rooms is that every one of us, without exception, has an interesting life story to tell and yet we rarely get the chance to be heard. All of us have had dreams which have been frustrated and diverted; and all of us have had to overcome hardships we haven't looked for and make decisions. Inside, we are powered by the same set of mundane emotions which we don't always recognise until someone points them out. If we don't give vent to them in appropriate ways they can come out in destructive ways – anger particularly.

It's easy to ridicule the self-help/therapy/personal development industry. It takes many ludicrous forms; can be painfully self indulgent; and is too often accessible to the people who need it least, the middle-class, privileged or comfortably off. Too often therapists are people who think that talking is a way to self-awareness or else they are ego-maniacs or religious fanatics. But we shouldn't write off the principles behind this mad circus; rather we should apply them more widely. The dictum that if you want to change the world you should first change yourself, sounds trite but it should be taken to heart by everyone, especially those entering politics.

Things are at least as good as they were

Things are not what they were, by definition, and they never will be again; but that's not to say they are any worse just because you think they are.

Of course, pop music is all derivative, manners have gone to pot, television has long passed its golden age, artists have nothing more to say, the young are not revolutionary enough etc. But as you get started on your list of gripes about the modern world, you might like to note that:

1. Every age says more or less the same and fails to see the novelty and value that is before its eyes.

Ancient Athenians were nonplussed by the wisdom of Socrates which his biggest fan, Plato, turned into a philosophy to which western thought has been nothing more than a footnote.

No one thought much of the Impressionists when they were getting going – the name they were given was not meant as a compliment.

For jazzmen, popular music stopped progressing in the 1950s; for flower-children it stopped progressing when Dylan went electric and the Beatles split up; for punks it stopped progressing when the music business started making a profit out of alienation; for Britpoppers it stopped progressing when Oasis and Blur put their egos before the indie cause. To bring the story up to date, ask any hip-hopper on the streets why pop has stopped progressing.

2. Nostalgia often makes our memories inaccurate – either that or we don't really know what we want.

Take tennis: in the 1970s we complained that the sport had been overrun by tantrum-tormented bad boys and we insisted that rules were adapted to enforce good behaviour. Now we ask why the players have such insipid personalities and have become machines for winning who live cleanly and with unnatural self-control and spend most of their time guarding their media image. Is that an improvement or not?

Oldies make up their minds as youngies, and refuse to change them. The world moves on but they don't want to move on with it. The best two lessons we can learn before we perch on a bar stool and preach about life in the golden age of our youth are:

- The establishment of any age is composed of laurel-resting, has-beens who are hopeless judges of the new talent which will have an impact in the future.

- If you can't see originality, creativity and dynamism you're not looking in the right place. It is unlikely to come from the same source or in the same area of life as previously.

Thinking

You can forget the rest of the book, if you want, and just mull over this: *if we can only think straight, all will be well.*

We keep getting told that we are possessed of the most marvellously over-capacitated, under-used organ inside our skulls and it's a great shame that there is still a lot of truth in Bertrand Russell's lament that "most people would die sooner than think; in fact they do so."

Science doesn't fully understand the mechanics of the brain, and we're not really sure how mind and consciousness relate to it, but we do know that thinking is a skill which can be learnt and taught.

The uncontested guru in the field is Edward de Bono who is most famous for introducing the idea of lateral thinking – a creative way of coming at a problem from the side when storming it from the front doesn't work.

Although, de Bono has written extensively about thought in a style which could not disconcert anyone and spent his life lecturing and promoting his work, his ideas have still only been taken to heart by a fraction of the human race. The core of de Bono's philosophy is that we can act more effectively and achieve more or what we want if we would only *think*:

> "Our software for thinking, which we inherited from the Greek Gang of Three – Socrates, Plato and Aristotle – is about truth, logic, argument and analysis. It's excellent, in the same way that the rear left wheel of a car is excellent. But it misses out on creativity,

design and perception - 90 per cent of errors of thinking are errors of perception, not logic."

We can solve the most intractable problems if we can learn to wear de Bono's 'six thinking hats'; switch from our right/wrong mentality to seeing 'beyond yes and no'; and adapt from our accustomed, limiting 'rock logic' to the far more flexible 'water logic'.

The great thing about thinking is that we all do it from the moment of birth (perhaps before) but we are rarely encouraged to improve our skills or learn new ones. De Bono's 'system' of thinking is surely an example of human knowledge whose power we underestimate and which needs to be taught in schools, alongside maths and languages, and adopted in politics. Perhaps in the future 'thinking consultants' will sit round the table at peace negotiations and moderate world debates, such as the current one on climate change, which is showing signs of conventional mental gridlock.

Sources

All of Edward de Bono's books, but especially *The Use of Lateral Thinking* (1967) and *Six Thinking Hats* (1985)

Transitions

Politics, like everything else, seems to go in fashions and while once there was a headlong rush of countries into the paternalistic arms of totalitarians and dictators, today, thankfully, the main flow is the other way, towards democracy and the freedom that it entails.

The transition between the two systems of government, however, isn't always easy. To some extent each country has to find its own route and it's difficult, if not impossible, to impose solutions from the outside, as has been found in Iraq.

Fortunately, though, there are some universal lessons being learned which can be applied, with adaptations, to any country going through political cold turkey. Spain, in particular, has good advice to pass on. Shortly after Franco died in 1975 the monolithic apparatus of repression that he had spent four decades assembling was peaceably dismantled by common consent and Spaniards look back almost with astonishment at how well the transition went. Today, it's hard to believe that less than thirty years ago Spain still languished outside mainstream European society.

"First lay the foundations of the future, then turn to tackling the past," Timothy Garton Ash, professor of European Studies at Oxford University, advises countries which are setting up as democracies. It is important to address the past but not too soon and too quickly: it must be done from a firm constitutional base.

To immediately start persecuting members of the old regime risks perpetuating the conflicts of the past; rather there must be an amnesty with people from the past government given the chance to prove they can function in new ways under democracy.

The past, however, must be re-examined and judged as soon it can be without reviving old divisions. South Africa's Truth and Reconciliation Commission is generally agreed to have been a success in giving a hearing to both perpetrators and victims, but the arts also have a large part to play in unravelling the complex moral conundrums that everyone has to face in a system which deliberately proscribes freedom.

Meanwhile, democracy must make explicit provision for ethnic groups and sub-nationalities that were excluded from power in the past but even then it can take time for old grievances to die out – as witnessed by the continuing problem of Basque terrorism originating in northern Spain.

At some point, the past must be consigned to the past but thereafter each new generation must be reminded about its history and taught to be jealous of its hard-won liberty.

Sources

Cultural Amnesia: Notes in the Margin of My Time, by Clive James (2007)

The Magic Lantern: The Revolution of '89 Witnessed in Warsaw, Budapest, Berlin, and Prague, by Timothy Garton Ash (1990)

The New Spaniards, by John Hooper (1995)

Violence

It's easy to get the impression that we live in a more violent world but our perception of actuality can be distorted by our fear – or the cynical determination of those in politics and the media to make us fearful.

Any statistics can be challenged and those to do with risk and probability must always be treated with caution and are always subject to local variations – anyone who has lived through a war or been the victim of a violent crime may find it hard to find comfort in the larger picture.

But the facts seem to show that there are fewer violent conflicts than there once were and that the world, in general, has become less dangerous.

The Human Security Report, published in 2005 by a group of researchers based at the Simon Fraser University in Vancouver, Canada, concludes that there has been:

> "a dramatic, but largely unknown, decline in the number of wars, genocides and human rights abuse over the past decade... the single most compelling explanation for these changes is found in the unprecedented upsurge of international activism, spearheaded by the UN, which took place in the wake of the Cold War."

The report writers note that human security is not the same as national security, a distinction our leaders often fail to make.

Chris Anderson of TED also believes that violence is diminishing:

> "Percentage of males estimated to have died in violence in hunter gatherer societies? Approximately 30%. Percentage of males who died in violence in the 20th century complete with two world wars and a couple of nukes? Approximately 1%. Trends for violent deaths so far in the 21st century? Falling. Sharply."

Historical comparisons are useful, says Stephen Pinker, to remind us that we are, in general less brutal:

> "Cruelty as popular entertainment, human sacrifice to indulge superstition, slavery as a labor-saving device, genocide for convenience, torture and mutilation as routine forms of punishment, execution for trivial crimes and misdemeanors, assassination as a means of political succession, pogroms as an outlet for frustration, and homicide as the major means of conflict resolution – all were unexceptionable features of life for most of human history. Yet today they are statistically rare in the West, less common elsewhere than they used to be, and widely condemned when they do occur."

We don't know what has gone right, says Pinker, because we're more interested in asking ourselves "why is there war?" instead of "why is there peace?" There are probably many answers: battle fatigue after two world wars and totalitarian experiments; the spread of democracy with its non-violent methods of preventing confrontation; our better understanding of psychology; the increase in communications making our fellow human beings seem real to us; wider and stronger trading links; improved living standards that we are reluctant to put in jeopardy even temporarily in order to fight a war. Or perhaps we're at last getting the message that violence produces victims but no long-term winners.

Sources

Human Security Report: www.humansecurityreport.info

A History of Force: Exploring the Worldwide Movement Against Habits of Coercion, Bloodshed, and Mayhem, by James Payne (2004)

Wonder (and wonders) of the world

We're overloaded with sophisticated electronic
distractions and entertainments and can download an
image of any major art work and/or piece of
monumental architecture on earth to our virtual
desktops, but thankfully there are still sights that can
put the gawp back onto our seen-it-all, know-it-all faces.
Even if you pack your bags tonight and start travelling
tomorrow you won't see all the wonders that survive (or
are being built) during your lifetime; or, to phrase that
more positively, you will never run out of things to see.

Only one of the Seven Wonders of the (Ancient) World
still stands: the pyramids at Giza. In 2000 a campaign
was launched to replenish the list with seven 'unofficial'
wonders of the present day: structures which are
"human-built and in an acceptable state of
preservation".

The result may say more about our taste for pseudo-
democratic soundings than about intrinsic value, but the
final shortlist of 21 contenders in this archaeological
beauty parade would still make a fairly good itinerary
for anyone with time on their hands. Unfortunately,
anything we regard as wonder these days is likely to be
a tourist attraction but at least that usually means there
is a degree of preservation.

The new wonders of the world were chosen from the
following list (★ marks the winners).

☆ Acropolis, Athens

☆ Alhambra, Granada, Spain

☆ Angkor, Cambodia

★ Chichen Itza, Mexico

★ Christ Redeemer, Rio de Janeiro

★ Colosseum, Rome

☆ Easter Island statues

☆ Eiffel Tower

★ Great Wall of China

☆ Hagia Sophia, Istanbul

☆ Kyomizu Temple, Kyoto, Japan

☆ Kremlin/St.Basil, Moscow

★ Machu Picchu, Peru

☆ Neuschwanstein Castle, Füssen, Germany

★ Petra, Jordan

☆ Pyramids of Giza

☆ Statue of Liberty, New York

☆ Stonehenge

☆ Sydney Opera House

★ Taj Mahal

☆ Timbuktu, Mali

There are many possible variations to the game of choosing wonders and you can make your own must-see lists which avoid the crowds and the need to shell out for air fares, hotels and admission charges. You could make a list of the seven sights most worth seeing in your own country (or even region or city). Or you could go in search of natural wonders: landscapes without ticket barriers. Then there are modern wonders, some combining original form with functionality, others merely examples of how clients of top architects like to show off: London's 'Gherkin', Dubai's Burj al Arab hotel, The Guggenheim Museum in Bilbao etc.

Alternatively, you could make a list of the seven places that have the most hold over the psyche of contemporary man, perhaps:

- The Vatican
- Jerusalem
- Las Vegas
- Manhattan
- The White House
- The Kremlin
- The remains of the Berlin Wall

Even more interesting is to play down the importance of scale, cost, visitor numbers and role in history and emphasise instead the capacity a place has to stimulate our curiosity, to teach us something and leave questions hanging in our heads that we don't feel the need to answer.

For the ape with itchy feet who finds it hard to sit still and contemplate his surroundings, you could compile a list of symbolic trajectories and methods of movement: the pilgrimage trails, railway lines, tunnels, canals, metro systems and air routes that have most changed our lives: the Moscow Metro, Channel Tunnel, trans-Siberian railway and so on.

There are many non-geographical directions this 'wonders' business can be taken in, too. The only limit is our imagination. Instead of places, we could concentrate on inventions, scientific discoveries, artefacts, works of art, political events, or even ideas that we visit via the internet and inside our own brains.

Sources

New 7 Wonders Foundation: www.new7wonders.com
1001 Natural Wonders: You Must See Before You Die, by Michael Bright (2005)

World government

I used to think that a world government would be A Good Thing, but I'm starting to reconsider that verdict. Now I see that I was imagining an enlightened, multi-coloured legislature of cool-headed sages converging on International Island, each thinking about what would be in the best interests of humanity without regard to the self-centred demands of his own tribe, race, religion, country, company, Swiss bank account etc.

I admit I was naïve and I have toned down my political dreams. The political experiments of the 20th century have left me wondering how a world government could be set up which would be safe, free and democratic. Imagine voting for the Global Parliament only for it to be taken over by a global dictator.

But don't we still need some fount of supranational decision-making that can iron out our differences and stupidities between nations; that can step in when a superpower gets full of itself; that can remind us that human rights should be placed above the designs of all governments?

The answer is a cautious yes. "We are living with nineteenth and twentieth century government structures for twenty-first century problems," says the economist Jeffrey Sachs and it could be argued that the nation state is an outmoded concept in these days in which capital flits across the globe at the speed of a fibre optic pulse.

If we have learned anything about political decision making and public administration, it is that each operation has its appropriate level. Sometimes power is most effectively exercised by a parish council but there are decisions which need to be taken at the highest level, which at present, nominally, is the highly imperfect United Nations. The UN has achieved considerable successes but inevitably it takes a lot of flak for being a toothless organisation with high ambitions.

However, we should aspire to perfect the supranational organisation or organisations we need to carry out functions that seem to be beyond the scope even of the last surviving superpower. If illegal wars can be condemned; if excessively polluting countries can be brought into line; if dictators can be ostracised; if war criminals can be brought to trial; if poverty with all its associated problems can be tackled at a global level - if all this can be achieved only by some kind of planetary forum, then that's what we need to have.

Sources

A Global Parliament - Principles of World Federation, by Christopher Hamer
Ourtopia, by Garrett Jones (2004)

Worse, *things could always be*

This is an old optimism stand-by motto, sometimes shortened by the British to "mustn't grumble". For most in the developed world it is undoubtedly true at any time in our lives; but you have to think it rather than say it or else the nearest pessimist will transform it into the equally true, "things could always get worse".

Even an optimist might admit that it takes an effort of will in hard times to believe that the not-bad is better than the not-good, and to be thankful for it. After a day in which you are fired and come home to an unexpected tax bill on the doormat, go out for a meal with your boyfriend/girlfriend only to be dumped and left to pick up the tab; and then wait for the last late-night bus which not only fails to stop but drives through a deep puddle and drenches you from head to foot, you might want to remind yourself that you have not been:

- ☠ Hung, drawn and quartered
- ☠ Skinned or burned alive
- ☠ Press ganged as a galley slave
- ☠ Sold into prostitution
- ☠ Committed to a lunatic asylum even though you know you are sane
- ☠ Ordered to charge a battery of field guns armed with nothing but a sabre

Note: this can be a difficult concept for spoiled children to grasp so don't waste your breath trying to explain it to them.

... the end of the world

If you are reading this, the end of the world probably hasn't happened yet. The chances are it won't happen in the foreseeable future and there is a possibility that it won't happen at all.

People have been predicting the end of time since the beginning of time. Nostradamus and Mother Shipton were two of the most famous doom-decriers but they were both fairly woolly in their prophecies. Many lesser seers have drawn on all sorts of 'hard' evidence (numerology, the Book of Revelation, the Great Pyramid etc.) to prove that the end is nigh and most religions have a eschatological stance of their own which is open to interpretation. None of these people have been even remotely right so the odds are pretty good that all non-scientific predictions will prove similarly inaccurate.

We should, perhaps, distinguish between the end of the universe, the end of the earth and the end of us. We're likely to be the shortest lived of the three and we're certainly the most vulnerable and the most stupid. Nuclear war or climate change could eradicate us as a species but let's assume that human ingenuity and instinct for survival means that we don't finish ourselves off. What else do we have to fear?

More bizarre ideas for the end of civilisation or the Earth have included the earth falling into the sun, the moon crashing onto the earth, a comet or meteorite strike, alien invasion and pole shift – by which Africa moves to the north pole and Antarctica to the equator. Well, any or all of these things might happen but there are no contingency plans you can make except perhaps to store a few provisions in a cave somewhere on a high mountain and hope for the best.

But what about the universe – how long has that got to live? The answer depends on what it weighs. Not to get too technical, the end of Everything depends on the value of the density parameter, Omega (Ω). If omega is greater than 1 we live in a closed universe and sooner or later all matter will try to cram itself into the same point of space-time in a 'Big Crunch'. If omega is less than 1, we live in an open universe which will go on expanding forever. There's still a chance that 'universal heat death', a 'Big Freeze', or the 'Big Rip' (in which everything disintegrates into elementary particles) would get us, depending on how well or badly phantom dark energy behaves. If omega is exactly equal to 1 we live in a flat universe which will behave similarly to an open one. Current measurements put omega at 1 or less, so we have a chance it will never end. There is also the possibility that we live in one of infinite number of multiverses (a parallel universe) and that ours might be of an infinite lifespan.

But even if the universe is heading for the 'Big Crunch', we may not be. In 1994 Professor Frank J. Tipler proposed the theory of the Omega Point* which states that as we get nearer to the end of the universe there will be such a phenomenal amount of energy available that the capacity of computers will increase faster than time

---

* I don't want to spoil a good story so I'll say this in small print: some scientists regard this theory as nonsense. But does it really matter?

runs out. Hence we would have an infinite amount of subjective time to enjoy, whatever was happening to the real universe. We will almost certainly have transferred our consciousnesses to some very clever machine by that time so we won't much mind if the whole experience is simulated rather than real; it will be the ultimate in widescreen, surround-sound home entertainment.

Because we will have such phenomenal computing power available we will be able to recreate anyone who has ever lived (or raise the dead, if you prefer). So we can run the history of humanity over and over again forever, fast-forwarding through the boring bits and pausing while you are being born (again) so that you can make a cup of tea. And if that's not a reason to be optimistic, you're difficult to please.

Sources

The Physics of Immortality, by Frank J. Tipler 1994

Sources

Many books and websites are referred to in the text or as footnotes at the end of the relevant sections. Sometimes, also as footnotes, I have suggested books for 'further thought': works which I have not drawn on directly but which will provide greater detail on the subject and which will, I hope, provoke more ideas than I have had space to cover.

I must make it clear that I do not necessarily agree with all sources I refer to and I would not expect their authors to agree with me. They may or may not consider themselves optimists – I cannot claim to speak for them – and I have often summarised, simplified or selected their arguments to fit my own context.

In addition to the works cited in the main body of the book, I am particularly indebted to those listed below, of which I have made generalised use, both for information and as the starting points of many trains of thought:

- *The Improving State of The World: Why We're Living Longer, Healthier, More Comfortable Lives on a Cleaner Planet,* by Indur M. Goklany (Cato Institute 2007, www.cato.org).

- *The Impossible Will Take a Little While: A Citizen's Guide to Hope in a Time of Fear,* edited by Paul Loeb (www.paulloeb.org)

- Wikipedia (en.wikipedia.org)

- The Edge (www.edge.org), a website published and edited by John Brockman. In January 2007, the World Question Center asked 160 'third culture' thinkers, 'What are you optimistic about?'

- *Bursting at the Seams,* by Jeffrey Sachs, director of the Earth Institute at Colombia University. Reith Lectures 2007, broadcast on BBC Radio 4 (www.bbc.co.uk/radio4/Reith)